John Lyons' The Making of a Perfect Horse

Veterinary Care

For The
Perfect Horse

ISBN: 1-879-620-57-X

Belvoir Publications Inc.
Box 2626
75 Holly Hill Lane
Greenwich, CT 06836 USA

Kellon, Eleanor V.M.D.
Veterinary Care for the Perfect Horse
Kellon, Eleanor V.M.D.
and the editors of John Lyons' Perfect Horse

ISBN. 1-879-620-57-X
1. Horses - Training   2. Horsemanship   3. Horses

Manufactured in the United States of America

John Lyons' The Making of a Perfect Horse

Veterinary Care

For The
Perfect Horse

Eleanor Kellon V.M.D.
and the editors of John Lyons' Perfect Horse

Belvoir Publications, Inc.
Greenwich, CT

Contents

Preface

It doesn't matter if our horse is 12 hands or 17 hands, if he's a pure-bred or an over-the-fence bred, a backyard pet or a top competitor, we love him and want to give him the best of care. In fact, I often say that my horses are spoiled — and I intend to keep them that way. I'm sure that's how you feel, too.

Back when Adam was alone in the Garden, God gave the animals to him and expected him to take good care of them. While our barn may not look like Eden, we have inherited that same responsibility, and with it comes the great joy and pleasure of providing for our special partners.

Good care involves more than just throwing feed over the fence. It involves monitoring our horses for potential health or soundness problems, as well as giving them regular preventive care, like vaccinations and deworming, to help keep them healthy. It also involves taking care of them on a daily basis — providing shelter from the weather, cleaning out their stall and giving them fresh water, feed and good grooming—- even on the days that we don't feel like doing it. Our animals give us so much back in love and enjoyment.

May we always be guided by our Creator in our lives and as we care for our perfect horses.

John Lyons

Your love. O Lord, reaches to the heavens, your faithfulness to the skies. Your righteousness is like the mighty mountains; your justice like the great deep. O Lord, you preserve both man and beast. How priceless is your unfailing love!   *Psalm 36:5-7*

Section I

Veterinary Care
For The Healthy Horse

1

What's Normal?
Know Your Horse's Vital Signs

*Knowing what was "normal" saved the horse
of competitive trail rider and judge Barbara Madill.
Here's how to tell what is normal for your horse.*

You can't pinpoint what it is, but your horse doesn't seem quite right. Is it a figment of your imagination, or is there really something wrong? It isn't like him to be last into the barn for his afternoon grain, and it certainly isn't like him to leave nearly half of his small ration. Usually, he is finished with his meal and terrorizing his less thrifty neighbors in the stalls to either side before you reach the end of the barn, but today he ambles out behind the others.

You turn him and his companions out into their customary pasture by the barn. He usually rushes to make sure he doesn't miss a single blade of grass that might have grown while he was in the barn.

Checking his stall, you find several small deposits of much-wetter-than-usual manure. Glancing out to the pasture, you see him lie down. He doesn't roll or look back at his side as if he were in pain. He just lies there, his muzzle resting on the ground.

The other horses are wandering about, nibbling their way up the hill. They look fine. You walk out to your horse, halter him and encourage him to rise. Normally, you would never see this horse lying down except to roll in the dustiest spot possible after a bath. He makes no objection to being led back into the barn alone.

You collect a thermometer and a stethoscope from your tack trunk. His temperature is 100.4°, his pulse rate 56 beats per minute and his respiration 40 breaths per minute, all higher than his normal. You call your vet. She tells you that the outside temperature is still above 85° and that it is quite humid, and thus the readings you have given her are within the normal range.

You remind her that this is the horse she jokes about being half dead because his pulse and temperature are always low. You also remind her this horse recently returned from an area where cases of Potomac horse fever are frequent. The vet and you decide she had better come have a look.

By the time she arrives, your horse's temperature has risen to 102°. He seems mildly uncomfortable and has been up and down several times. Deciding that this is not a simple case of colic, the vet praises you for not having administered any medication. She shares your concern that the symptoms could be the early stages of Potomac horse fever, or worse yet, salmonellosis.

While she waits for lab results on the blood she drew, she arranges to admit your horse to the nearest veterinary hospital, hours away. If the horse is suffering from a bacterial infection, such as salmonellosis, he'll need hospitalization to have a chance of survival.

Barbara Madill, an experienced long-distance rider, knows this scenario well, because it happened to her. Because Barbara knew her horse's normal ranges of pulse, respiration, temperature and general behavior, and because her veterinarian knew that "normal" for most horses was not "normal" for this horse, the story had a happy ending; in fact, the horse went on to a successful long-distance career, including winning two grand championships in 100-mile competitions.

What is normal?

When Barbara first started long-distance competition, "normal" was whatever the veterinarians judging called normal. Score sheets rarely had the actual readings on them, and the judges often used an "A," "B," "C" scoring system and wrote "normal" or "high" for pulse and respiration.

After the organization of the Eastern Competitive Trail Ride Association (ECTRA) in 1970, the pulse and respiration data from sanctioned rides helped establish the current baseline used for scoring purposes: **a pulse of 44 beats per minute and a respiration of 24 breaths per minute. Horses are expected to recover to these numbers within 20 minutes of finishing a ride**, as opposed to the old days when final recoveries were recorded an hour or more after competition.

Because rapid breathing is one of the ways that horses get rid of excess body heat, anytime a horse's respiration rate stays much

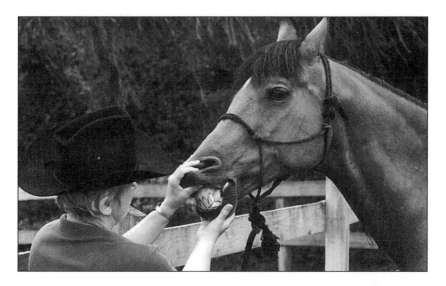

Lift the horse's lip to note the color of his gums and the capillary refill time.

higher than his pulse, his temperature should be checked. In hot, humid weather, the high temperature of a horse unable to cool by sweat evaporation can be life threatening. You should expect to find a pulse in the 30s to low 40s, respiration in the 20s and rectal temperature between 100° and 101° Fahrenheit. On a particularly hot and humid day, you might expect a higher pulse and respiration, but the temperature should still be under 102°. Even with low humidity, heat should be taken seriously.

Gathering resting data

A horse is in resting state when he's relaxed standing hip shot with ears in neutral, like you watching the average TV show. To evaluate your horse, pick a time and situation you can duplicate easily during your normal routine.

Ideally, use a well-lit location for your evaluation (if not in his stall, perhaps the barn aisle, or somewhere you can tie him, since you may not have a helper). Bring a paper and pen so you can record what you find, watch with a second hand or a display in seconds and, ideally, a stethoscope. You can usually buy a stethoscope at the pharmacy for under $10. Most people have a hard time determining the pulse without one.

Count the heart rate for 15 seconds and then multiply it by four to get the beats per minute (pulse rate).

Look at the horse in order to document his normal posture, markings and conformation. Does he stand squarely or with his hind legs camped under him or out behind him? If he rests a hind leg, is it always the same one? Does he have lumps, bumps or swellings anywhere on his body or white hair in the saddle area? How is each hoof shaped?

It's like examining a rental car before you take it out on the road. You are not looking for good or bad, just documenting what you see.

Pulse

With your stethoscope, find the spot where the heart beat is strongest, usually a couple of inches above and behind the horse's left elbow. Listen to the rhythm for about 15 seconds before you start timing. Most horse's hearts make a "lub dub" sound for each beat, with the accent on the "dub," but there are many variations in a healthy horse. If your horse is particularly fit or truly resting, You may still have trouble occasionally identifying the beat and keeping with the rhythm, especially if there are any flies around. Every wiggle the horse makes can interfere with the stethoscope's contact, and the occasional gurgle from his digestive system can be disconcerting.

Even if you hear the heart beat as soon as you put the stethoscope on the horse, be sure to hold still and wait a few seconds before starting your count; even just the touch of the stethoscope to the horse will momentarily speed up his heart.

Count the beats for 15 seconds, then multiply the total beats by four to get the reading per minute. Count each "lub dub" as one beat. A 30-second test would provide a more accurate rate per minute, but it is hard to keep with the beat for that long.

Some people are skilled at counting the pulse using the artery that runs along the jaw. Some can get a good count using the "digital" pulse behind the fetlock, or the pulse along the underside of the tail. If you can't feel the jugular or digital pulse, try finding the pulse where the neck and chest join.

BECAUSE RAPID BREATHING IS ONE OF THE WAYS THAT HORSES GET RID OF EXCESS BODY HEAT, ANYTIME A HORSE'S RESPIRATION RATE STAYS MUCH HIGHER THAN HIS PULSE, HIS TEMPERATURE SHOULD BE CHECKED.

Respiration

Counting breaths per minute can be tricky, but with patience you'll get an accurate rate.

Watch the horse's flank, and time the in-and-out movement for 15 seconds, each in-and-out registering as one breath. This sounds easy, but with the slightest distraction, the horse may sniff a couple of times, messing up the count.

Don't be surprised if the horse seems to hold his breath for a number of seconds and then takes a few short breaths. You may have to time several 15-second sessions to get an accurate respiration rate.

A really fit horse, in cool weather, can have a resting respiration as low as eight breaths per minute. If the rate is low, you may want to time for longer than 15 seconds.

Hydration

There are several indicators of how well hydrated the horse is, but the easiest is the "skin pinch." Because a horse's skin can vary in elasticity, test three points on the base of the neck and shoulder. After grasping a fold of skin and twisting ever so slightly (rarely will a horse object), release the skin and count the seconds it takes for the crease to disappear. The skin of a well-hydrated horse will flatten out in less than a second, a little longer for an older horse. Any horse whose skin stays puckered for three or four seconds will probably show other signs of dehydration as well.

Before you do this test for the first time with your horse, try it on yourself. Lightly pinch a little skin on your hand in the web between your thumb and first finger. See how it snaps back into place? That's what you're looking for.

Another sign of hydration is capillary refill. That's a fancy way for saying how long it takes for the horse's gums to regain color after pressing a finger against them. Lift the horse's lip and gently press with one finger on his gums just long enough to leave a "fingerprint." Immediately start counting. You want to see the color return almost immediately. Make a mental note of how moist and slippery the mucous is.

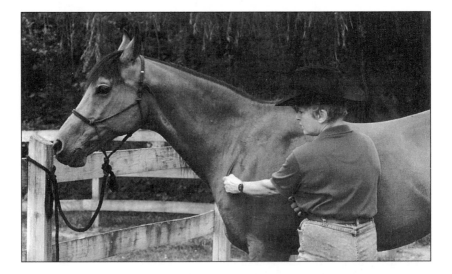

For an accurate skin-pinch test, the horse's head should face straight ahead, and you should "pinch" several places.

Mucous membrane color

When you are doing the "cap refill" test, observe the color of the horse's gums. They should be pink or yellow-pink. Check the membranes at the corner of the horse's eye as well. These tissues should also be moist and pink unless he's been working in dust, has an allergy, is sick or approaching fatigue. Checking the eye takes a little practice. Press at the corner of the eye just enough to see the mucous membranes. The horse's acceptance of this will be valuable if you ever need to medicate his eyes.

Body temperature

If your horse accepts being handled everywhere on his body, taking his temperature is never a problem. However, leave temperature-taking until last in case it disturbs him. If he clamps his tail down and acts nervous, you'll need to handle him more before you place the thermometer.

Tie one end of a piece of string through the hole in the end of a veterinary thermometer and the other end to a small alligator clamp.

Shake down the thermometer until the bulb reads below 96°. Lubricate the thermometer with petroleum jelly.

To take his temperature, raise the horse's tail and hold it slightly off to the side. Insert the thermometer about two or three inches into the rectum and clip the alligator clamp

After years of temperature-taking, Barbara's horses automatically lift their tails when she asks.

to the horse's tail (so that the thermometer does not get lost inside the horse's body). Even with that precaution, stand close by for the minute and a half it takes to take the temperature. Before using it on another horse or putting it away, be sure to clean the thermometer with alcohol.

Record keeping

Once you have determined what is normal for your horse, keep a record of it handy, along with an identifying photograph, a copy of a recent Coggins test, the list of his current vaccinations and any other information that would be important, should others be caring for the horse. You can keep a copy of this information in your truck console and/or post a set in the barn, perhaps in a zippered plastic bag to protect it from flies and dampness.

If you own a mare, start to keep track of when she is in heat. It's easy if you keep a calendar in the tack room and just make a mark when you notice her in season.

You may also want to include also a brief notation regarding your horses' personalities, their strong likes and dislikes, and any quirks that could be problematic should someone else be caring for them. If your horse normally rolls after dinner, that would be important to record as normal for him, because seeing him roll might alarm someone feeding for you on a weekend you're out of town. ■PH■

2

Diagnostics A To Z

With our hard-earned dollars and our horse's health at stake, it pays to know what we're paying for when the vet says a diagnostic test is in order.

The common and not-so-common diagnostic tests and techniques used in equine medicine can be confusing. Here's a glossary of the tests most frequently performed and their approximate costs. A farm call or exam fee is often added to the procedure fee.

AUSCULTATION: The veterinarian uses the stethoscope to listen to (auscult) various areas of the horse's body. Beginning with the head, when the stethoscope is placed over the sinuses, a soft sound of air movement may be heard. The veterinarian may tap on (percuss) the sinuses and can tell by the tone (high-pitched or dull) whether or not there is fluid or blood in the sinuses (see percussion).

Auscultation of the lungs can yield much information. The exam begins by listening over the trachea (windpipe) in the neck, then proceeds to the chest. The larger airways (bronchi) are heard at about the top third of the chest, while sounds from deep in the lungs are heard low and toward the end of the ribs. Diagnosing lung problems with a stethoscope takes considerable experience, and a thorough examination may take 15 minutes or longer (it's a big chest!). The types of sounds heard give clues to what the nature of the problem may be.

Auscultation of the heart can determine the actual heart rate. When that is compared to the pulse rate felt over an artery in the legs or face, the veterinarian can detect any beats that are not effective at

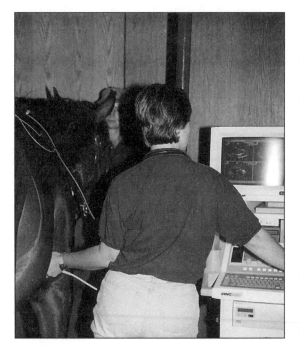

Echocardiograms scan the horse's heart and produce an internal picture on the screen that works like radar.

pumping blood. (The heart rate is greater than pulse rate.) Common arrhythmias (disturbances of heart rhythm) can be detected this way without the need for an EKG. The veterinarian may also hear "extra" or "split" heart sounds, which indicate there are abnormal pressures in the lungs or large blood vessels.

Murmurs are diagnosed with the stethoscope, and by noting where they occur in the heart cycle, the veterinarian can often decide which heart chambers and/or heart valves may be abnormal. Even the intensity of the heart sounds and such things as how large an area can be covered on the chest while still hearing heart sounds give valuable information about such matters as fluid surrounding the heart.

Listening to the abdomen is also helpful when horses seem to be colicky. The experienced veterinarian is familiar with the types of sounds normally heard, how often they are heard and how loud they are. Abnormal sounds, fewer-than-normal sounds or a combination of both, depending on where you listen, indicate possible problems. Cost under $50.

BONE SCANNING: See SCINTIGRAPHY.

ECHOCARDIOGRAM: An echocardiogram is a special form of ultrasound (see ULTRASOUND) used to evaluate the heart. Echocardiograms give a three-dimensional view of the inside of the heart, including all the valves and chambers, the major vessels in the area and the walls inside the heart.

The device that emits the ultrasound waves is either passed along the chest wall or placed into the horse's esophagus. The image the veterinarian sees looks similar to a radar-screen image on a ship. Structural problems, such as diseased valves or holes in the heart's interior walls, are immediately obvious.

The echocardiogram can also tell you if the heart is functioning well or working harder than normal and if the heart muscle is strong. Cost over $100.

EKG (ELECTROCARDIOGRAM): This is called an EKG and not an ECG (although ECG is sometimes used) because the abbreviation is taken from the German spelling of the test. Sensing electrodes, called leads, are positioned along the horse's chest wall and record the electrical activity of the heart. That information is printed onto a strip of paper as a series of peaks, with two major peaks for each heart beat.

By looking at the distances between the peaks, the veterinarian can tell if the electrical system of the horse's heart is working normally. The size and direction of the peaks give information about how well the heart muscle is functioning. The overall pattern tells whether or not the rhythm is normal.

An EKG can also determine how well the muscle contracts, how strong it is, whether the chambers are normal in size and even if the horse has a severe electrolyte abnormality. Cost $50 to $100.

ENDOSCOPY: Endoscopy is the examination of interior portions of the body using a "scope" — more properly, a fiberoptic endoscope, a specialized camera. The interior of an organ or area is lit by an intense light source at the end of the scope, and the picture is transmitted along the tiny interwoven fiberoptic elements inside the scope, going to the viewer's eye and, usually, a viewing screen.

Endoscopy is routinely used to get a good look at the structures in the nose, sinuses and throat. Endoscopes can also be passed down into the lungs themselves, into the esophagus or farther (depending on the length of the scope).

Endoscopes are also frequently used to examine the urinary tract and the mare's reproductive tract. Veterinary surgeons sometimes use them to examine the structures inside the chest or abdomen. By passing special instruments through particular channels located in the endoscope, it is also possible to obtain biopsies or culture specimens and to sometimes perform minor surgeries, such as removing small tumors. Cost $50 to $100.

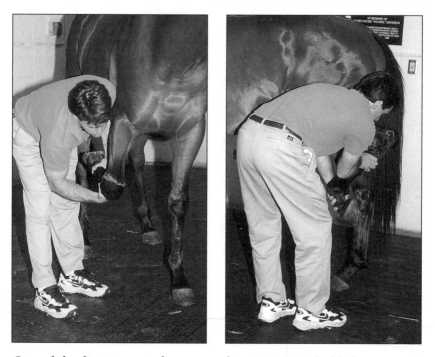

One of the first steps in lameness diagnosis is to hold the suspect joint in a stressed/flexed position for a minute or so, and then jog the horse to see if lameness is worse.

FLEXION TESTS: The flexion test is done to stress a joint in order to exaggerate any lameness originating from that joint. In a flexion test, the veterinarian holds a joint (or joints) in a flexed position for up to 60 seconds. When the leg is released, the horse is jogged off and observed. The test is considered to be positive if the lameness is worse after flexion, and negative if the lameness is unchanged.

Occasionally, a horse will actually seem to be less lame after a flexion test. This usually occurs when the flexion test has actually been mildly positive, but the horse was showing lameness in one or more other legs before the flexion. With the new discomfort caused by the flexion test, the horse may go more evenly and appear to be sound.

Great care must be taken when performing flexion tests to avoid stressing more than one area at the same time. For example, when flexing a hock, the stifle will often also be flexed. If the leg is held too high when doing a hind-leg flexion test, the hip joint will be stressed at the same time. Cost under $50.

Variations of flexion tests

Variations of flexion tests — that is, tests that also aim to stress an area in question but do not do it by flexion per se — are also used in lameness diagnosis. With the feet, a good diagnostic test is to stand the horse on a block of wood with the toe elevated for 60 seconds, then jog him off. When the toe is up on the block, the structures in the back of the leg are stretched. This exaggerates any deep flexor tendon pain or navicular pain. Horses with low ringbone may also be more lame after this test.

Another variation, used for detection of shoulder, hip or sacroiliac pain, is to pull on the leg. In testing for shoulder soreness, the front leg is pulled back and held for approximately 60 seconds, then the horse is jogged off. (Conversely, pulling the leg forward will often help horses with sore shoulders to move more freely when they are jogged off.) With hip and sacroiliac pain, the leg is grasped and pulled to the front, then to the back and then away from the body. Pulling the leg forward is usually the most successful at eliciting a response, but all positions should be tried before calling the test negative.

NERVE BLOCKS: Nerve blocks are generally done when it is difficult to tell from observation and examination where the problem or problems lie. Much like the dentist numbs a section of your mouth, the veterinarian injects a local anesthetic to numb a superficial nerve, usually in the horse's lower leg, to block out painful sensation coming from an area of suspected lameness.

Each nerve in the body supplies a specific area with sensation (and impulse to move). If the horse goes sound after the injection, the nerve block is said to be "positive," meaning the site of lameness was identified as within the structures that were supplied by the blocked nerve. The nerve blocks start low in the leg — first the foot, then pastern and fetlock, and so forth.

Nerve blocks are a relatively safe and routine procedure. The most common complication is some bleeding, as blood vessels run close to nerves. However, this is easily controlled. Costs vary depending upon the time needed and number of spots that have to be blocked; assume anywhere from $50 upward.

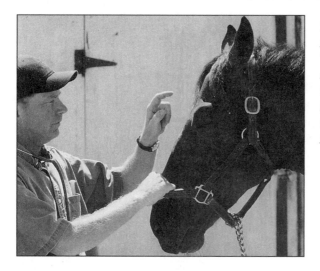

This veterinarian is tapping/ "percussing" the sinuses to see if they sound clear (hollow) or filled with some material (dull).

OPHTHALMOSCOPY: Ophthalmoscopy is examination of the interior structures of the eye using an ophthalmoscope. The ophthalmoscope can be used to examine all depths of the eye, from the structures at the level of the pupil, down to the lens, then all the way to the optic nerve and retina in the back of the eye. The ophthalmoscope provides detailed views of all these structures and important information regarding such things as the health of the optic nerve (the nerve that supplies vision), the blood supply to the retina, any damage to the retina or infections deep in the eye. Cost under $50, often more if done by a specialist.

PALPATION: While breeders typically associate the word "palpation" with the reproductive exam of a mare, palpation means simply carefully feeling an area of the body. Careful palpation of a leg can detect subtle swellings or differences in temperature that indicate a problem. Firm palpation will often disclose areas of tenderness before a lameness or visible signs, such as swelling. Palpation of muscles detects subtle differences in tone and areas of sensitivity. Cost under $50.

PERCUSSION: Percussion is the technique of applying short, sharp taps to an area and listening for the tone produced (with or without the assistance of a stethoscope). Just as different types of drums produce different sounds, different amounts of fluid, solids and gas under the area percussed will produce different tones on percussion.

Percussion is used over the chest to map out the area. Large areas of dullness indicate that the lung beneath is either filled with some material, collapsed or has a layer of fluid overlying it. In the abdomen, percussion will produce characteristic tones over normal air/fluid-filled intestine and different high-pitched "pings" when the bowel beneath is gas-filled. Cost under $50.

PERITONEAL TAP: A peritoneal tap is the process of obtaining a fluid sample from the abdominal cavity. Peritoneal taps are done in colic cases or any time a problem is suspected in the abdomen.

To obtain the fluid, the veterinarian either makes a small incision and forces a blunt-tipped "needle," called a cannula, into the abdomen or carefully inserts a regular needle. This is a delicate procedure, since you do not want to puncture a piece of intestine. The fluid collected can be checked for signs of inflammation, infection, liver disease or rupture of an organ. Cost usually under $50, more with extensive tests on the fluid.

RADIOGRAPHS: X-ray machines send radiation through the part of the horse's body being radiographed, and the image is impressed on a film plate. X-ray images are much the same as negatives from a regular camera. Black areas have allowed virtually all the radiation to pass through. This is the case when the beam goes through air or fluids like blood. Dense structures, such as bone or metal, appear white — allowing little radiation to pass right through. Variations of gray indicate the density of the matter.

X-rays are still the first choice in diagnostic tools for evaluation of bone problems. However, when you look at an X-ray, you may be seeing the bone as it was about six weeks previously in many cases.

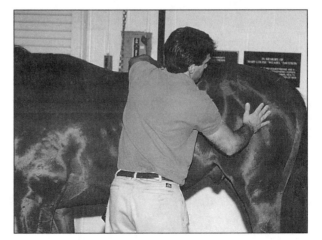

One of the experienced vet's most sensitive tools is still simple palpation — feeling for heat, skin tension, bumps or anything that may not seem normal.

This is because changes in bone that have not yet had calcium deposited in them are "invisible" on X-rays. This is why a complete lameness examination, history and use of nerve blocks must always be done with the X-rays. More sensitive diagnostic tools such as SCINTIGRAPHY (bone scans) and XERORADIOGRAPHY are sometimes suggested to help clarify the meaning of X-ray findings. Cost about $20 per film.

RECTAL EXAMINATION: Also known as rectal palpations, rectal exams are used for the diagnosis of abdominal problems and to assess the reproductive status of a mare. Rectal examinations are helpful in determining the possible causes of abdominal pain (although a precise diagnosis may be impossible) and helpful in determining if the horse may require surgery.

To perform a rectal examination, the veterinarian inserts his plastic-gloved, lubricated arm into the rectum of the horse. In colic cases, it is possible to feel loops of intestines, as well as the kidneys (at least one), bladder, uterus and ovaries on rectal examination. If an area of intestine is blocked, twisted or is not moving its contents normally, gas and fluid will accumulate in front of the blocked or

abnormal area, and the veterinarian will find large smooth loops of intestine that feel like giant water balloons. If the distended areas are sitting low in the abdomen, the veterinarian may feel tightly stretched tissues (called "bands") that are being pulled by the heavy, distended loops.

Impactions can often be felt on a rectal examination. Such things as tumors, enteroliths or abscesses may not be felt if they are large,

Stethoscopic exam is particularly helpful in determining "gut" activity in cases where colic is suspected.

as heavy structures tend to fall to the bottom of the abdomen. However, the veterinarian may feel bands or notice some distention of the bowel caused by that type of a problem.

Rectal examination of mares is done to determine if the mare is pregnant or to determine if she is ready to be bred. When doing a rectal examination to estimate optimum time for breeding, the experienced veterinarian will carefully check each of the ovaries to determine if they contain a follicle (fluid-filled sac with the egg inside) that is at, or close to, its mature size and ready to release the egg.

Rectal examination for pregnancy, although still performed, is rapidly being replaced by ULTRASOUND examination, since ultrasound is more accurate and can detect pregnancy earlier. Cost under $50.

SCINTIGRAPHY: Sometimes referred to as nuclear imaging, scintigraphy is a technique that measures the uptake of a radioactive material by various tissues in the body. In equine medicine, it is almost exclusively used to evaluate bone and joint problems.

In scintigraphy, the horse receives an intravenous injection of a material that has a high attraction to the tissues to be examined (in most cases, bone) and has a radioactive material attached to it. In the first few minutes after injection, the radioactive dye concentrates in the blood stream. Shortly after this (15 to 20 minutes), the radioactivity moves into the other tissues of the body. Finally, it concentrates in the bone.

The horse's entire body (or only the area in question) is "scanned" with a device that counts the radioactivity (much like a Geiger counter) and maps it out onto a viewing screen. Any area that has a high metabolic rate (such as growth plates or fractures) or a high degree of inflammation (such as infection, arthritis, new fracture) will show increased uptake.

Obviously, scintigraphy is a sophisticated diagnostic technique and not one likely to be performed in your backyard. It is primarily used in cases where standard diagnostic techniques, such as flexion tests, nerve blocks and routine X-rays, do not give a satisfactory diagnosis.

Bone scans also may be recommended as a "first-line" diagnostic tool in horses who seem to have problems in more than one location simultaneously (more than one leg, more than one joint) or if a problem is found that could involve more than one joint (i.e., OCD — osteochondrosis dessicans). Cost over $100.

SPINAL TAP: A spinal tap is the insertion of a needle into the area surrounding the spinal cord for the purpose of obtaining a sample

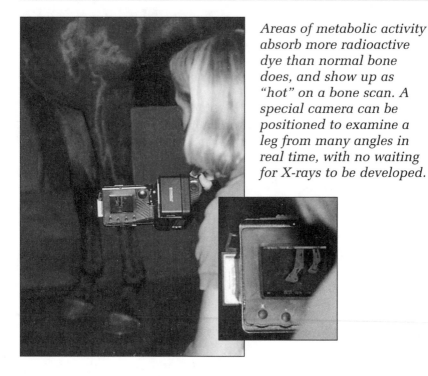

Areas of metabolic activity absorb more radioactive dye than normal bone does, and show up as "hot" on a bone scan. A special camera can be positioned to examine a leg from many angles in real time, with no waiting for X-rays to be developed.

of cerebrospinal fluid — the fluid that bathes the brain and spinal cord. Fluid is needed for diagnostic tests (cell counts, protein content, cultures, cytology) when there is a suspicion of trauma or infection to the brain or spinal cord (i.e., EPM).

In most cases, the needle is inserted in the lumbosacral space. As you follow the spine back toward the rump, you can feel that the upward projections get progressively smaller. At a point just in front of a line drawn connecting the hip bones, there is a dip or indentation. This is the lumbosacral space.

The horse is usually lightly tranquilized, and the skin at the needle insertion site may be anesthetized first with a local anesthetic to reduce movement by the horse when the needle is inserted. If the horse is extremely unsteady or very uncooperative, general anesthesia may be needed to perform the procedure safely.

On rare occasions, the veterinarian may decide to obtain fluid from an area closer to the brain. In this instance, the needle is inserted at the space between the first and second cervical vertebrae, high in the neck close to the base of the skull. This requires the head be flexed tightly and is done under general anesthesia only. Cost is approximately $100 (more with general anesthesia), with tests being extra.

THERMOGRAPHY: Thermography is a technique that detects areas of underlying inflammation by picking up differences in the surface temperatures overlying such areas. A sensitive temperature probe is steadily passed over the areas of the horse's body (usually on the lower leg) in question. With the most sophisticated units, the information obtained can be transformed into a picture where the temperature of different areas is depicted as a specific color, from black for the coldest/background to reds and yellows for the hottest.

Thermography is not particularly helpful in reaching a specific diagnosis — all it tells you is that a certain area is receiving more blood flow than another, presumably because of active inflammation and/or a healing response. However, it is a fairly simple test and helpful in locating the most "active" sites on a leg. For example, a horse may have evidence of a bowed tendon, osslets and joint puffiness all on the same leg. Some of these problems may be old and inactive. Thermography will help the veterinarian to focus on the areas of active inflammation. Cost $50 to $100.

THORACIC TAP (tapping the chest): A thoracic tap is the procedure of inserting a needle, and usually some tubing, into the chest to obtain samples of fluid and to drain abnormal collections of fluid.

A small area is "blocked" with a local anesthetic and a tiny incision made. A blunt-ended "needle," termed a cannula, is inserted through the muscles between ribs and into the space between the chest wall and the lungs. Tubing is then inserted through the cannula to collect or drain fluid. The fluid obtained can be tested for evidence of inflammation or infection, even tumor cells. Cost $50, more depending on tests run on the fluid.

ULTRASOUND: Ultrasound is a diagnostic technique similar to radar used in submarines and airplanes. It measures how sound waves pass through or are reflected when they hit objects of different density. While X-rays are most useful for looking at heavy, hard tissues such as bone, ultrasound can diagnose problems with the soft tissues of the body, such as muscles, tendons, ligaments and organs.

Tendons and ligaments can be viewed by ultrasound to detect disruption in their normal structure. The examiner looks for two things: collections of blood or fluid, which indicate a recent injury in that area, and changes in the normal pattern of the tissue. Fluid or blood appears as a dark "hole" in the substance of the tendon.

Disruption or disorganization of tendon tissue is more difficult to uncover. The tissue is normally woven together and organized in a

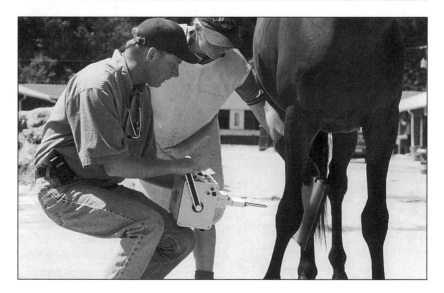

Portable X-ray machines can take excellent pictures of the lower joints and save you from having to take the horse to a clinic.

characteristic pattern — like the herringbone weave of fabric. Changes in this repeating pattern show up where a tendon was injured recently and has not repaired itself, as well as in areas of old injury where the repair was not perfect.

In reproduction, ultrasound is most often used for detecting pregnancy. Ultrasound can also be used to detect abnormalities of the uterus or ovaries, such as tumors, and can help determine if a follicle (egg-containing sac) is present and how close to rupturing it might be. Cost $50 to $100.

XERORADIOGRAPHS: Xeroradiographs are a specialized form of radiography. Both xeroradiographs and routine X-rays require radiation to expose films. X-ray images are produced by a chemical change in the film; xeroradiographs by an electrical change.

Xeroradiographs produce a white/gray picture on a blue background. They are superior for demonstrating soft tissue changes and minute details of the bone. For example, xeroradiographs are used for detecting tiny fractures and will show changes such as bone cysts much better than conventional radiographs. Use of xeroradiography equipment generally involves a greater exposure to radiation than routine X-rays and is not suitable for portable/farm use. Cost somewhat more than conventional X-rays, usually $25 to $50 per film. **PH**

3

Why A Coggins Test?

*Most of us know we need a current Coggins test
in order to transport or show our horses,
but many don't remember why.*

When Dr. Leroy Coggins was born, his parents probably never imagined his name would become a household word — at least in households with horse ownership! Since Dr. Coggins developed the diagnostic test for equine infectious anemia (EIA) in 1970, it has been adopted worldwide as the standard screening method for detection of horses who harbor the EIA virus.

Coggins tests, which confirm that a horse is free of this virus, are required or requested in a wide variety of circumstances — to show, for entry onto large farms, as part of prepurchase examinations, for entry onto racetracks, entry into sales and to legally transport a horse across state lines or in or out of a country.

Equine infectious anemia, sometimes referred to as "swamp fever," is a viral disease that can affect any member of the horse family (donkeys, mules, horses and so forth).

This virus attacks the horse's blood cells. Its favorite targets are the macrophages, large white blood cells that scavenge for invading organisms or other foreign material. Viral multiplication results in severe anemia, a drop in the platelet count and fever. Other common symptoms, depending on the stage of the infection, are a depressed attitude (usually accompanies the fever), edema of the legs and loss of condition.

EIA is caused by a virus in the retrovirus family. More specifically, it is a lentivirus, which is sometimes termed a "slow virus."

Dr. Leroy Coggins speaking on EIA and the test that bears his name.

Members of the slow-virus group cause a slow, steady downhill course. During the long time that the infected victim remains alive, viruses periodically multiply, and the animal is capable of spreading the disease.

There are a few "firsts" about the EIA virus that are important. It was the first virus of its group **proven to be transmitted by biting insects.** This, of course, greatly increases the danger of spread of the disease, since **no horse-to-horse contact is required.**

Another important "first" is a little more complicated. This was the first persistent viral infection proven to have "antigenic drift." **Antigenic drift is the ability of the virus to change the characteristics of its outer covering.**

When the horse's body detects a viral invader, it "reads" the sequence of amino-acid proteins in the virus's outer coat and begins to manufacture antibodies specifically designed to form a close fit with that sequence. These antibodies then neutralize any viruses in the blood stream that fit that pattern. Viruses that remain "hidden" inside cells are not affected by the antibodies. However, for the viral infection to stay alive, the virus must multiply and break out of the cells, making it vulnerable to the antibodies again.

With the EIA virus, antigenic drift makes it possible for the virus to develop a new strain of itself that is different enough to avoid detection by the horse's antibodies. **The horse's immune system must then go to work all over again manufacturing new antibodies to match the new strain.** It takes about two weeks for the antibody level to become sufficiently high to seriously threaten the invader. Of course, two weeks is plenty of time for a virus to multiply over and over again, making it virtually impossible for the horse's antibody system to catch up.

Therefore, antigenic drift is important for two reasons: First, it provides a way for the virus to undergo repeated — and theoretically unlimited — cycles of multiplication that are long enough to keep the infection well established in the horse before his immune system can catch up. Second, **antigenic drift makes it extremely difficult, nearly impossible, to develop a vaccine.**

Horse AIDS?

There are many striking similarities between the EIA virus in horses and the human HIV virus that causes AIDS. They share the same classification — lentiviruses.

- *Both produce slowly progressive disease.*

- *Both target blood cells.*

- *Both defy attempts to produce a vaccine.*

- *Both viruses are spread by contact with virus-laden blood and cannot be spread through the air or by simple contact with the victim.*

In fact, there are so many similarities that diagnostic tests for one can often also detect the other. This has not gone unnoticed by those involved with AIDS research, and the EIA virus is considered to be a good research model for AIDS. This could accelerate the pace of research on the EIA virus and lead to some breakthroughs in our understanding of it.

AIDS and EIA are two different viruses, so of course, you don't have to worry about catching AIDS from an EIA-positive horse.

Stages of the disease

When a horse first becomes infected with the virus, he is in the "acute phase." This is his first exposure to EIA virus, so he has no protection. **All horses in the acute phase are sick, but the symptoms vary widely.** Some become severely ill and die within two to three weeks. However, most horses receive only a small dose of the virus from an insect bite, possibly even only one insect bite, and do not show such dramatic symptoms. There will be fever, but it may be present for only a relatively short time and can easily be missed. Some degree of depression and possibly loss of appetite will occur. The whole episode could easily be interpreted as a "cold."

However, much more is going on inside the horse's body. Before he can mount an effective antibody response, the virus multiplies. It has been stated that as little as one cc (milliliter) — which is one-fifth of a teaspoon — of blood from a horse in the acute phase contains enough virus to infect one million horses! During this acute period, a "Coggins test" will be negative, since antibodies have not reached a measurable level as yet. **Most horses will become "positive" within 10 to 14 days of infection. However, their symptoms will likely have subsided long before that time, and there will be no seeming need to run the test.**

DURING THE LONG TIME THAT THE
INFECTED VICTIM REMAINS ALIVE, VIRUSES
PERIODICALLY MULTIPLY, AND THE ANIMAL
IS CAPABLE OF SPREADING THE DISEASE.

Once the horse's antibodies have reached a good level, the virus will be forced to retreat back inside the horse's blood cells to "hide." There, it will become inactive but not dead. Stress, such as another illness, severe weather, heavy exercise, a long shipping, movement to a new location and so forth, may be enough to trigger the virus to begin multiplying again. Antigenic drift comes into play here, and the newly formed viruses will be different enough from the original ones that new antibodies will form.

Horses that have this going on inside their bodies are said to be in the chronic stages of EIA. Some horses will show symptoms of anemia, easy bruising, low platelet count, weight loss, poor appetite, depression and edema during each wave of virus multiplication. Coggins testing at this stage will be positive.

A certificate indicating a negative Coggins test is required at all sanctioned competitions.

Most horses that are EIA-positive are in a category called "in-apparent carriers." They rarely, if ever, show flare-ups of the disease, but they continue to have antibodies and live virus in their bloodstream. What makes some horses sick and others apparently healthy carriers is not known, but it undoubtedly has to do with how efficient their immune system was at developing at least some antibodies that are effective against multiple strains of the virus. When a horse is an inapparent carrier, or in chronic cases that are between bouts of obvious illness, there is estimated to be only about a one-in-six-million chance that a bite from a horse fly will pick up enough virus to infect another horse.

This one-in-six-million chance is obviously low and is the reason there is much resistance to the idea that an EIA-positive horse should be humanely destroyed or kept in strict quarantine for his entire life. Unfortunately, there is no way to predict which horses will remain inapparent carriers and which could be triggered by stress to go into a relapse of the disease in the chronic infection category, which is why all positive-Coggins horses are considered potentially dangerous to other horses.

In summary then, the odds of an infected horse who appears healthy continuing to live a healthy life are probably fairly good for that individual animal. Owners, understandably, are unwilling to part with their friend because of the off chance he might become ill someday. **However, if the horse does become stressed and viruses begin to multiply at high rates again, the chances of his being a threat to other horses in the area are very, very high.**

The government's stance regarding EIA is that **every Coggins-positive horse poses a potential threat to other horses and must be either euthanized or quarantined for the remainder of his life.** (Quarantine restrictions are up to the individual states to define.) This may seem an extreme sentence, especially for horses who are clinically normal, but the potential risk they pose to other horses, at unpredictable times, and no real hope of a vaccine combine to create this policy, which serves the best interests of all horses.

FYI

During the Coggins test, blood from the horse is put into small wells on a test tube plate, which is covered with an agar/gel containing the antibodies (an immunodiffusion test). The blood proteins slowly spread through the gel and, if EIA proteins are present, they react with the antibodies, forming a visible line. This is a "positive" test, meaning the horse is infected with EIA. ▣

4

Vaccines: A Short Guide For The Horse Owner

*If you've ever wondered how vaccines work
and which ones your horse really needs,
our report will help clear up the confusion.*

In brief, a vaccination is a deliberate exposure of the horse either to a disease-causing organism (virus or bacteria) or to some portion of a disease-causing organism in hopes of causing an immune response that will protect the horse from future infection.

What do vaccines do?

Building immunity against a disease is like building an army to fight a particular invader. When a virus or bacteria is introduced to the body, the body recognizes it as a foreign invasion and goes on alert. The body manufactures soldiers (antibodies) of a special size and shape who fight the disease when it first appears, and who will recognize any reappearance of it. That's why someone who has had measles rarely gets measles a second time. If they are exposed to measles, their antibodies fight off the new measles invasion, often without the person feeling anything.

A vaccination is actually a very small invasion — just enough of the disease that the body can begin the process of making antibodies to that disease, so that if a real invasion hits (the disease itself, not just a vaccine,) there will be sufficient antibodies to fight the disease and protect the homeland (the person or animal). The first smallpox and polio vaccines were actually deliberate infections of people with a very small dose of the bacteria/virus, small enough

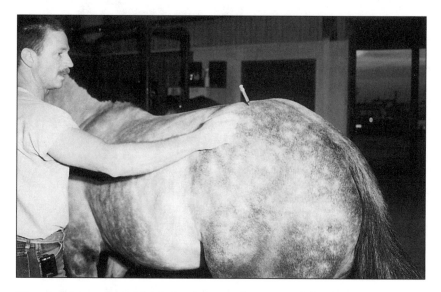

Vaccinations placed high in the muscle mass of the rump can cause problems if an abscess develops, since it will not readily drain.

(hopefully) not to kill or cripple them. The person would, essentially, have a very mild case of the disease. Once recovered, they were immune to a more serious infection.

Both human and veterinary medicine have come a long way, and today the closest we come to that admittedly risky practice is a small number of vaccines containing viruses that have been partially "inactivated" so they do not cause a serious infection. Such vaccines are labeled "modified live," which simply means they contain live organisms but in a form that will not produce dangerous disease. **The advantage of modified live vaccines is that they result in a stronger immunity than other vaccines; that is, the body recognizes the invasion as a little more serious and thus makes more and stronger antibodies.** Their disadvantage is a stronger reaction in general (higher fever, possibly even a mild case of the disease that you are trying to prevent), and reactions at the site of the injection are likely to be more severe (swelling, abscess formation, pain).

Most vaccines contain either dead organisms ("killed" vaccines) or only a portion of the organism that is known to induce an immune response (i.e., the cell wall or selected proteins). These vaccines are safer than modified live, reducing to virtually zero the likelihood of actually developing the disease and reducing the severity of reactions.

Do vaccines work?

Vaccines vary widely in their effectiveness. It should be stated right up front that no vaccine is 100 percent effective. Improper storage and handling of vaccines, their improper administration and factors within the horse that impair his ability to mount an effective immune response cause decreased effectiveness. **Stress factors such as malnutrition, parasitism, recent infection of any type, recent transport, heavy exercise, rapid growth, serious wounds, lactation (nursing a foal), and even extremes of weather can affect the horse's response to even a very good, properly stored and administered vaccine.**

In addition to the vaccine and the horse, the nature of the organism you are vaccinating against plays a role. Vaccine makers carefully weigh the effectiveness of a vaccine against its safety. Obviously, if the vaccine prompts a full-blown infection, the horse will develop more immunity than if he just has a mild infection, but the full-blown infection is exactly what you are trying to prevent by vaccinating him in the first place. The vaccine maker modifies the organism in the vaccine so that it does not produce as much damage as the natural infection would — otherwise, the vaccine has no value. In the process of altering the organism to make a safe vaccine, the level of immunity drops. However, even vaccines that provide less than 100 percent protection or require multiple, closely spaced injections to be effective almost always provide the horse with enough resistance to the disease that symptoms will be lessened, recovery will be quicker and complications less likely.

Timing combination vaccines

When using combination vaccines, (vaccines that combine protection for two or more diseases into one vaccine) timing may be important. For example, vaccines containing encephalitis should be given in the early spring, before the start of mosquito season (twice a year where bugs exist year-round). Vaccines for flu and "rhino" should be given at least two weeks before the start of any period of high exposure (i.e., show season or planned trail ride). These requirements may make combinations unsuitable for your individual circumstances. Your veterinarian is the best person to consult for advice on the suitability of combination vaccines and for guidance in timing all vaccinations.

Who should vaccinate?

It is no secret that owners and trainers can purchase vaccines directly in many states. For vaccines that are administered by simple intramuscular injection, there is no particular danger to the horse if someone other than a veterinarian gives these vaccines, assuming the person is knowledgeable about proper injection technique, uses a sterile needle and syringe, cleans the injection site correctly and follows the manufacturer's instructions about storage. However, there are several reasons why it is advisable to have your veterinarian vaccinate your horse:

■ There is always the potential for adverse vaccine reactions, whether immediate allergic-type reactions or delayed vaccine reactions, such as a high fever, or complications at the site of the injection. The veterinarian will have the necessary prescription drugs to treat these reactions.

■ Some veterinarians limit their practice, including availability for emergency calls, to those clients who use them for complete health care — including vaccinations. Most veterinarians do a brief physical exam of a horse before they vaccinate him, and the value to you as a horse owner of having the vet observe his overall health may be far above the savings you would have by vaccinating the horse yourself.

■ In some states, it is against the law for anyone but a veterinarian to administer a vaccine.

■ Some vaccines are available only through a licensed veterinarian.

Tetanus/Lockjaw

This disease occurs when a specific type of bacteria gains access to a deep wound, where it grows and produces a toxin that attacks the nervous system. Tetanus is **fatal,** and horses are extremely sensitive to the toxin. The tetanus-causing bacterium is found virtually everywhere, including in manure, making exposure a constant threat. **Every horse should be vaccinated for tetanus.**

Encephalitis

There are three types of viral encephalitis that can attack horses: Eastern, Western and Venezuelan. **The horse becomes infected by** bites from mosquitoes carrying the virus. Eastern and Western encephalitis are well established in this country; Venezuelan makes an appearance only on occasion, usually in states close to the Mexican border. **Encephalitis is a serious, potentially fatal infection of the brain.** Horses that survive may have permanent defects. Again, **all horses should be vaccinated for encephalitis.**

Rabies

We all know that the rabies virus causes a fatal infection of the nervous system. Rabies is caused by a bite from infected animal, often a bat, raccoon or skunk. **A horse with rabies often goes undiagnosed for a prolonged period of time and can spread the infection to humans (i.e., by contact of body fluids with broken skin, such as a cut on the hand).** Rabies is well established, even epidemic, throughout the United States, and ALL horses need annual rabies vaccinations.

Potomac horse fever

Potomac horse fever is a disease characterized by fever, depression, diarrhea and founder. It is largely confined to specific geographical areas (i.e. along the Potomac River, where it got its name), in areas of moderate climate and close to rivers. Some farms also have a higher incidence than others in the same area. Owners of horses in moderate climate areas should check with their veterinarian and/or local extension agent about the advisability of vaccination in their area.

Rotavirus diarrhea

Rotavirus causes a severe, potentially life-threatening diarrhea in young foals. **It appears that the virus is carried by the mother (or probably another horse), who does not develop problems, but passes on the infection.** A vaccine has just been developed, and vaccination should be considered for all pregnant mares. Vaccinated mares then pass the antibodies to their foals in the colostrum (first milk). There is no geographical boundary for the disease, and even mares that are kept away from all other horses may have foals with Rotavirus diarrhea, since mares may carry the virus from the time they were foals themselves.

Botulism

Botulism is the same disease as caused in people by eating contaminated canned goods, and it is caused by the toxin of a bacterium related to the one that causes tetanus. Again, horses are highly sensitive to it, and a very high percentage die from the disease or its complications. Treatment with antitoxin is expensive, but prevention by vaccination is recommended.

Influenza

Horse flu and human flu are very similar diseases, both showing severe cold-like symptoms and high fever, bearing the risk of developing bacterial pneumonia and having periods when the virus mutates, causing epidemics to break out. **Because this virus can mutate easily, vaccines are often considerably less than 100 percent effective in preventing the disease, but can reduce the severity of the symptoms.** Any horse traveling (i.e., to shows or a new area) is at high risk, as is any horse stabled where there is horse traffic. Flu is most dangerous (as with people) to the horse that is very young, very old or under stress (i.e., performance, shipping, etc.).

Rhinopneumonitis

Commonly known as "rhino," this disease is the equivalent of our own "common cold." However, the rhino virus can also invade the nervous system, causing paralysis, and can cause abortion. The risk factors for rhino are the same as for influenza. Additionally, **all pregnant mares should be vaccinated, every two months throughout pregnancy.**

Strangles

Strangles vaccination is *not* done routinely but is recommended for horses at high risk of exposure (i.e., known contaminated premises, shipping around to competitions, breeding stock being shipped to breed or located on a farm with much traffic on and off the premises). This is at least partially because the risk of side effects from the intramuscular vaccine is so high (up to 30%). These include fever, loss of appetite, local swelling, muscle stiffness and abscess formation at the vaccination site. Protection is also not particularly good. Vaccines usually provide reliable protection from severe disease for only a few months and do not prevent the disease completely.

The newest strangles vaccine is designed to be delivered as a spray into the horse's nose, mimicking a natural exposure. The vaccine actually contains live Strangles organisms, but in a modified form that will not produce the disease. Intranasal vaccination has a very low incidence of side effects (a clear nasal discharge being the most common). Protection appears to last about as long as with the intramuscular vaccines.

The intranasal vaccine has not been approved for use in pregnant mares (although it appears to be safe in pregnancy). Part of the problem with the intranasal and pregnant mares is that it is not clear if antibodies in the blood (which are needed for the foal to get protection from the colostrum) are stimulated as well with the intranasal vaccine. It is therefore wise to use the intramuscular vaccine with mares who are close to foaling.

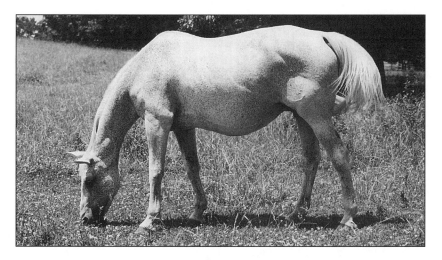

Pregnant mares have special requirements for the timing of their vaccinations. Because foals are born with immature immune systems, their initial protection from disease comes from the antibodies present in their mother's first milk, the colostrum. To provide the foals with optimal antibody levels, vaccinations should be administered two to four weeks prior to the anticipated foaling date. This schedule will also result in good antibody levels in the mare at the time she is likely to be taken for rebreeding.

Recommended vaccination schedule

Tetanus
> Two doses initially, one month apart.
> Yearly, may be recommended after an injury.

Encephalitis
> Two doses, one month apart.
> Prior to mosquito season; once a year if mosquito season is short, more often with long seasons or if traveling to a warmer area.

Rabies
> One dose.
> Yearly.

Potomac horse fever
> Two doses, one month apart.
> Every 6 to 12 months, depending on the area.

Botulism
> Three doses in initial series.
> Yearly.

Influenza
> Two doses initially, one month apart.
> Every two to six months during periods of high risk.

Rhinopneumonitis
> Two doses initially, one month apart.
> Every two to three months for maximum protection.

Strangles
> Intranasal: 2 doses initially, 3 weeks apart.
> Yearly to twice yearly.
>
> Intramuscular: 3 doses initially, 2 months apart.
> Yearly to as often as three to four times.
> Yearly in heavy problem areas.

Rotavirus
> Rotavirus vaccine is still being evaluated and is not yet on the market, but it can be obtained by licensed veterinarians. ■PH

5

Demystifying Deworming

Easy-to-use, low-toxicity deworming drugs have put the responsibility of deworming squarely into the lap of the horseowner. Everyone welcomes the savings, but how do you choose the correct dewormer?

Every horse should be dewormed on a regular schedule. Some natural-living proponents claim you should never use deworming drugs, that they are worse than the worms, that they cause more problems than they prevent and that the horse only needs natural levels of immunity, but the facts prove otherwise. The damage that parasites and their immature life forms can range from moderate to life-threatening:

■ Immature life forms may dig into walls of the intestine and/or migrate virtually anywhere in the body, including through the arteries, into the lungs, into the liver and kidneys, even into the brain.

■ Immature and/or mature intestinal parasites may bite/suck the wall of the intestine, leaving raw damaged areas and potentially causing loss of blood.

■ Large numbers of worms in key locations may cause obstructions and severe colic.

■ Damage to the intestine (irreversible) may prevent the gut from moving normally in some areas, resulting in anything from repeated bouts of low-grade colic to severe complications and a life-threatening colic.

■ Rapid release of numbers of previously dormant life forms (encysted small stronglyes) can make the horse so toxic that founder or death result.

■ A host of more minor symptoms related to poor digestion and faulty absorption of key nutrients, such as poor hair coat,

An easy way to hold the horse's head and guide the syringe into the right place is to hold the halter with the fingers of the right hand, and use the thumb to draw the corner of the horse's lips up. Make sure the horse doesn't have food in his mouth.

Set the dosage on the syringe, depending on the type of deworming syringe you are using. Hold the syringe in the left hand and slip the point of the syringe into the back of the horse's mouth, keeping the point low so you don't poke the horse in the roof of his mouth.

Steadily push on the plunger with the thumb of your left hand, until the medication is all dispensed. Continue holding your horse's head until he swallows, so he can't easily spit the drug out.

dull attitude, poor growth and an overly distended abdomen (often called a "hay belly") that is the result of abnormal amounts of fluid and gas in the bowels. Not every type of parasite can produce all this damage, but none of them are harmless. It may take weeks, months or years before a related-health problem develops, but the chance of having one is very high.

A horse's first exposure to parasites comes from his mother's manure, even her milk. Immature dormant forms of threadworms are triggered by late pregnancy and migrate to the mammary gland and appear in the mare's milk.

Roundworm exposure through the mare's manure begins with the foal's first tentative exploration of the ground. Roundworms are only a minor problem to the horse from about one year of age until his old age, when immunity often wanes and the horse is no longer as effective. This parasite

Rotectin 1 and 2 make up an easy-to-use rotation program.

adapts to the loss of its immature host by going dormant, lying harmlessly in the tissues — unless it is resting in a mare who happens to become pregnant. Hormonal changes in late pregnancy trigger the emergence of these worms, and they mature just in time to begin laying large numbers of eggs when the foal is born. It's a nifty system that's great for the worm but potentially disastrous for the foal.

Beyond roundworms and threadworms, a variety of other parasites lurk on and around every blade of grass that has ever been the resting site of another horse's manure. No deworming drug can kill every immature and adult form of every species of equine parasite with one treatment. And no management measures can guarantee complete removal of infectious life stages from a pasture.

Unless your horse is living under strict laboratory isolation conditions, he has worms and he will continue to be exposed to worms throughout his life. Whether you like the idea or not, even if your horse is rolling fat and has never had a sick day in his life, he has worms. But with a good program, effective control is indeed possible and at a cost that is far less than the cost of resultant health and performance problems if you don't do it.

A scoop a day keeps the worms away

An alternative to scheduling regular dewormings is to go with a daily dose of the drug pyrantel tartrate (Strongid C, Equi AidC with Strongid C). The advantage to the daily deworming drug is that mature/egg-laying worms are kept to a minimum, avoiding fluctuations in parasite burdens caused by seasonal variation, use of an ineffective dewormer (resistance) or failure to deworm frequently enough.

This schedule is not 100% effective, but those who endorse it claim this is really a benefit in that permitting a very low level of infestation is a stimulus to the immune system. The main drawback is that only adult forms are killed, so a horse exposed to a large number of immature parasites will likely suffer all the ill-effects of these life stages (migration through the tissues, development of encysted forms, etc.) unchecked. You will need to add seasonal dewormings for bots.

Daily deworming routines are most suitable for mature horses in a relatively stable environment, who are not likely to be exposed to large numbers of immature parasites. Most veterinarians recommend that you treat the horse with an intensive "purging" deworming before starting this program to eliminate as many immature and mature life forms as possible before going to the low-dose daily treatment. It is also best to start this type of program at a time of year when pasture levels of parasites will be low — either during a long hot and dry spell or in extremely cold weather.

When and how often

"When" in this case refers to the time of year and, in foals, the time of life. "How often" refers to the frequency of treatments, either on a year-round basis or during high-risk times.

To deal with foals first, much is in favor of deworming foals every 30 to 45 days for the first year of life. Foals are extremely vulnerable to intestinal parasite damage. Their immune system is not equipped to fight off the pests, so the pests are free not only to set up house undisturbed inside the intestines, but also to wander at will throughout the body. Many cases of foal pneumonia — and more than likely other lung problems that surface later in life, such as heaves and lung bleeding with exercise — have their root in parasite damage in the young foal.

Since we can only test for parasite eggs, and eggs are only produced after a worm has matured, there is no way to tell for sure how much of a parasite burden (immature forms) the foal has at any given time. Some modification to this rigorous deworming schedule can be made in special ultra low-risk situations and, depending on the type of dewormer used, but better safe than sorry should definitely be the guiding rule here.

With mature horses, there are two schools of thought regarding when and how often. The simplest approach recommends deworming at regular intervals (usually every two months) all year round, with some adjustments in choice of drug depending on the most prevalent parasite at certain times of the year and/or the parasite being present at a life stage that is vulnerable to deworming.

The second program is to concentrate dewormings around the time(s) of year when the parasite is likely to be actively laying eggs and existing in an infectious stage. In general:

- Deworm before grazing season to eliminate egg-laying adults.
- Deworm frequently during peak grazing season.
- Forget deworming when the weather is hot and dry.
- Deworm in the fall for bots and any stray other types.

This certainly makes sense, but it assumes cold winters with no grass growth and does not allow for general variation in weather patterns and possible contamination during milder winter months.

The best approach is to take the strengths of the two programs and combine them, using knowledge of the types of dewormers, to come up with a program that should work well all the time.

Ivermectin vs. Moxidectin

Who is the real winner? Ivermectin has a broader range of effectiveness than moxidectin, being effective against 34 different parasites and life stages compared to moxidectin's 23. Whether ivermectin is truly more effective than moxidectin against bots remains to be seen, but we can tell you that at least one stage — the larval form that invades through the mouth and causes mouth and tongue sores — is not affected by moxidectin, but is by ivermectin.

Moxidectin is a poor choice for foals when compared to ivermectin because it lacks activity over some key life stages of roundworms and threadworms. In fact, moxidectin is not approved for use in foals.

Moxidectin claims to suppress strongyle egg counts for longer than ivermectin, meaning you do not need to deworm as often. However, this is only true for the small strongyles — the ones moxidectin has better activity against in more life stages. When you look at the dangerous large Strongyles (the "blood-worms"), there is absolutely no benefit to using moxidectin over ivermectin.

Moxidectin's one clear advantage is against encysted small strongyles. This parasite used to be considered only a minor problem, but as ivermectin effectively limited large strongyle numbers while missing this key life stage of the smalls, the picture changed. It certainly makes sense to take advantage of this unique characteristic of moxidectin, and we would recommend you use this drug in the treatment that precedes the growth of lush spring grass and again toward the end of peak grazing season, as there is some evidence to suggest these worms are triggered to leave their dormant state during times of the year when weather conditions are most favorable to their survival.

Note: It has been suggested that horses who get "sick," colicky or go off feed after a deworming, especially with ivermectin, are doing so because the dewormers killed off essentially all parasites except for encysted small strongyles. The theory is that the encysted small strongyles then know that "the coast is clear" and will emerge in large numbers. While it is a possibility, there is essentially no hard evidence to prove this theory, and the older explanation — that they are getting sick because of the large number of dead worms — is just as likely.

The deworming drug options

Ivermectin (Zimectrin, Eqvalan, Rotectin I and Equimectrin) and moxidectin (Quest) are the two superstars of deworming drugs, controlling a wider range of parasites and more different life stages than other classes of dewormers. Ivermectin's list of controlled species and life stages exceeds moxidectin's. Extensive use of ivermectin is probably responsible for saving more horses from parasite-related colic and blood-vessel damage than any other preventative medicine measure in recent memory.

Moxidectin's drawback is that it is not effective against the immature life stage of roundworms that migrates extensively in foals, and it is also not effective against the life stage of threadworms that is transmitted to foals via their mother's milk. The drug is also not cleared for bots by the FDA, although more extensive studies in other countries suggest it may be almost as effective against bots. Like ivermectin, it is not effective against tapeworms.

Pyrimidine wormers (pyrantels — Strongid P, Strongid T, Rotectin II and Strongid C) are a separate class of deworming drug that is extremely safe and highly palatable. There is a pelleted form designed for daily administration for constant control (but not elimination) of worm burdens.

Among pyrantel's advantages is that it can be used in double doses (Strongid or Rotectin II) to treat for tapeworms. (This is an "extra label" use, not officially recommended or endorsed, but commonly used by veterinarians. Consult with yours first before doing this.)

The **benzimadazoles** — notably thiabendazole (Equizole), fenbendazole (Panacur and Safeguard) and oxibendazole (Anthelcide EQ) — are another broad spectrum and effective class of wormers, but the ones most likely to be associated with resistance problems.

Closely related, and with similar ranges of effectiveness, are the probenzimadazoles oxbendazole (Benzelmin, EQUI-CIDE) and febantel (Cutter paste). All are 95 percent-plus effective against adult large and small strongyles, pinworms and roundworms. Administering oxibendazole at 1.5 times the usual dose will kill threadworms.

Parasites have the potential to become resistant to not only any given member of the class, but also partially or equally resistant to other members of the class. This is called "cross resistance." One member, fenbendazole (Panacur or Safeguard), can be used like ivermectin or moxidectin to kill the dangerous immature forms of the large strongyle ("bloodworm").

Double doses are used for this purpose, for four or five days straight.

This "purge deworming"program is often recommended on large farms to treat incoming animals and make sure they will not contaminate the premises with parasites shortly after their arrival.

Piperazine (Wonder Wormer and Alfalfa pellet) is a narrow spectrum but safe drug, primarily of use in rotational worming programs for foals. It has good results against roundworms and small stronglyes, but is only 80 percent effective with pinworms and less than 50 percent effective against the dangerous large strongyles.

Sample deworming schedules

■ *PLAN I*
  Treat once with moxidectin, then
  with ivermectin every 60 days OR
  moxidectin every 90 days.

Advantages/Disadvantages: Ivermectin is effective for treatment of parasites in young animals and for bots. This plan will adequately control mature and immature forms of all major parasites. Ivermectin will not kill encysted small strongyles, but the number of parasites surviving to reach this stage will be small if deworming is done every two months. Does not get tapeworms. There are no known cases of parasites becoming resistant to ivermectin and therefore no need to rotate wormers.

Moxidectin is more effective at controlling small strongyles, now the No.1 parasite of horses. Does not get tapeworms.

■ *PLAN II*
  Moxidectin every 90 days OR
  ivermectin every 60 days,
  except in April and October, when you should
  use a double dose of pyrantel pamoate to
  guard against tapeworms.

Cost: Same as Plan I.

Advantages/Disadvantages: Adding the Pyrantel pamoate lets you rest easy about the possibility of tapeworms. Tapeworms do not represent a significant threat to every horse, although their potential to do so rises when you regularly use moxidectin and/or ivermectin.

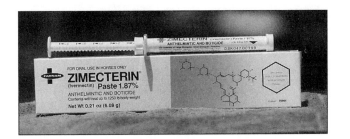

■ PLAN III — ROTATIONAL YEAR 'ROUND

January   Pyrantel pamoate
*(do a double dose if also
targeting tapeworms)*

March   Moxidectin
May   Ivermectin
July   Benzimadazole
September   Pyrantel pamoate
(can double for tapeworms)
November   Ivermectin

Cost: Lower than Plan I as pyrantel pamoate and the benzimadazole drugs are less expensive.

Advantages/Disadvantages: This program uses the strong points of each category to best advantage. Moxidectin in March will kill encysted small stronglyes before they can contaminate pastures during peak grazing season. Ivermectin in May gives you excellent control over mature and immature forms that are at their highest at this time of year. January, July and September are not particularly worrisome times for heavy pasture levels, so the other dewormers will do an adequate job of killing off stray adults. November is an excellent time to get rid of bots — use ivermectin. This program will not be as effective as Plan I if new, heavily parasitized animals are added to the group and contaminate the premises or if horses are being shipped out to areas that may be heavily contaminated. Avoid this problem by isolating new animals in a stall for seven days after arrival and treating with ivermectin, moxidectin or other larvicidal treatment plan. Never allow horses to graze or eat off the ground when away from home.

■ *PLAN IV — SEASONAL ROTATIONAL*

March	*Moxidectin*
April	*Benzimadazole*
May	*Ivermectin*
June	*Pyrantel pamoate*
	(double dose to also kill tapeworms)
August	*Benzimadazole*
December	*Ivermectin*

Cost: *Same as IV*

Advantages/Disadvantages: *Many parasitologists favor heavy deworming on a rotational schedule during times of peak grazing. This concentrates treatments when they are most needed and also avoids constantly exposing the parasites to drugs to which they might develop a resistance. The timing and drugs recommended takes into consideration their specific effectiveness against parasites most likely to be a problem at those times.*

Deworm a month or so before prime grazing season starts. This depends upon your location (February in southern states, March in more northern ones). Once the lush spring growth has started to come in and weather is becoming more balmy, deworm every three or four-weeks and continue this until temperatures become very hot and the ground begins to dry out. Then deworm one more time in late fall or early winter to clear out any remaining bots (ivermectin time). If you really have no true "winter" with dead grasses, this program may not be your best choice. Consult your veterinarian first. ■PH

6

The Value Of X-Rays

*X-rays are among the most commonly
employed diagnostic tools in equine medicine.
But, what can they actually tell us?*

Lameness problems are bound to crop up somewhere in the course of every working horse's life, often prompting the call for X-rays to be taken. While X-rays, technically called "radiographs," are useful, they are limited in what they can actually show and even more limited in how much they can tell about the future use of the horse — or even the source of a horse's current pain.

Radiographs show differences in density of the tissues being viewed. The object to be X-rayed is put between the X-ray machine and a photographic plate. The machine sends a beam of X-ray particles. The more dense the object, the fewer particles reach the plate. **Dense tissue, such as bone, allow few radiation particles to pass through to hit the X-ray screen. For this reason, dense tissue shows up as a white area on the developed film.**

In areas where virtually all of the radiation passes through, the film is black. **Thus, the air around the leg is blacker than any of the tissues in the leg.** Similarly, air inside the tissue, usually caused by gases produced in an infected pocket, will also appear black.

Whole blood tends to blend with surrounding tissues, although special views, such as taken to determine navicular disease, can make areas where blood vessels run through bone more apparent. Collections of edema fluid or serum (the fluid base of the blood, without blood cells in it) appear fairly black, more like air. Tendons and ligaments are difficult to make out clearly on X-rays, although

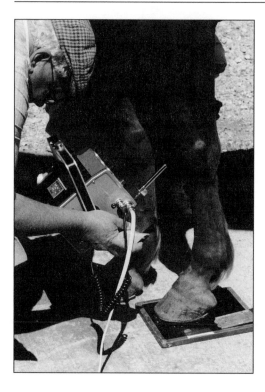

X-ray quality can be compromised if the technician, horse or plate moves while the shot is being made. And, like good photographers, veterinarians are careful about the positioning of the horse and plate, as well as movement.

their outline is often visible because they are a thick, dense type of tissue. Tendons, ligaments and skin layers appear as various tones of gray.

Small areas of calcium deposits, called calcification, often appear in locations that were previously inflamed, infected or injected with an irritating medication. We refer to variations from the ideal as "radiographic changes" or "changes."

What X-rays cannot show

Although X-rays show details of bone well, and are often used to diagnose arthritis, they have limitations. Changes in the cartilage surface, the joint fluid or the joint capsule are "invisible" on X-rays. Therefore, you may have a horse who is obviously lame and has arthritis with damaged cartilage, but his X-rays look normal. Similarly, a horse who has pain because of a sprained/strained or otherwise damaged tendon, ligament or joint capsule (the thick covering of tissue that surrounds joints and holds the joint fluid in place) may well have X-rays that look "clean" (negative).

With arthritis, which is often the main concern when joint X-rays are taken, such things as small chips broken off a bone or the formation of osteophytes or "bone spurs" are visible. Osteophytes are tiny build-ups of bone that appear as a fuzzy area along the edges of a joint's surface, indicating the bone has been irritated/inflamed. In more advanced cases, they appear as small spikes or teeth.

This occurs for several possible reasons: conformational abnormality that puts the edges of the bone in one or more locations too close together, damage/thinning of the cartilage cushion between bones, thinning of the joint fluid, insufficient production of joint fluid or even overextension or overflexion of a joint, as might occur during speed work or extreme turns on the haunches. In reality, usually more than one factor is at work in a joint, but the bottom line is the same — osteophytes indicate arthritis.

The problem with using the appearance of osteophytes to diagnose arthritis is that they take quite some time to appear, usually six weeks from the time the first injury or irritation occurred. **Therefore, when osteophytes are seen on an X-ray, they represent the result of a process that began at least six weeks before.** Since osteophytes themselves are not necessarily painful, the fact they are present does not guarantee that the joint is painful at the time the X-rays are taken.

Navicular disease

Navicular inflammation is a common cause of lameness, and X-rays are almost always used in making this diagnosis. X-ray changes consist of large "holes" in the navicular bone and the appearance of spurs (osteophytes) on the edges of the bone, where the ligaments that suspend it are attached. Spurring may occur on both sides, on only one side or be more obvious on one side than the other.

The holes seen on special views of the navicular bone represent channels in the bone that blood vessels travel through. When the area is inflamed, blood flow is increased, and the swollen vessels eventually cause the bone edges surrounding them to recede, widening the passage for the blood. As a horse ages, these channels normally become somewhat wider, which is why many radiologists classify them as "normal" or "not normal" for the horse's age.

Osteophytes, however, are not normal. They are produced when the navicular bone is subjected to increased concussion and vibration, such as work at speed, work over hard surfaces or from a foot that is too small to comfortably absorb impact forces. Osteophytes also form when the pull on the ligaments suspending the navicular bone is greater on one side than the other. This occurs when the foot surface is not properly balanced.

Enlarged vascular channels alone do not confirm a diagnosis of navicular disease, although they may strongly suggest it. A heel nerve block should be done to confirm the diagnosis. With osteophyte formation, the diagnosis is more solid, as any horse that has had enough irritation to this area to cause osteophytes to form will likely continue to have problems with pain from the navicular.

Founder

When a horse is suspected of having laminitis (founder), X-rays are important. With mild cases, caught and treated early, there may be no changes on X-rays. However, even slight movement of the coffin bone inside the foot (P1, the distal phalanx), commonly referred to as a "rotation," confirms a potentially serious laminitis diagnosis.

It is common to see a black area between the hoof wall and the edge of the coffin bone. This is a collection of serum/fluid that leaks out of damaged tiny blood vessels and causes quite a bit of pressure and pain (similar to when you injure a fingernail or toenail and have a pocket of blood under it). Veterinarians and farriers use the X-rays to determine how to trim the foot to line up the rotated bone with the hoof wall (remove toe, leave heels long).

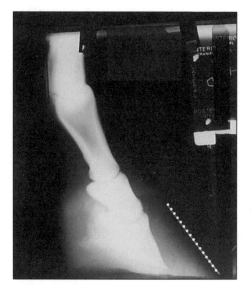

The bone inside the horse's foot (coffin bone) is normally parallel to the hoof wall (dotted line). This horse, having foundered, has a rotated coffin bone.

Standing the horse on a block allows the X-ray machine to be positioned directly opposite the horse's foot. The pin taped to the foot shows up as a white line on the X-ray, indicating the front edge of the hoof wall.

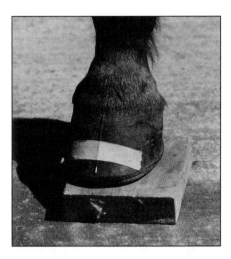

Ringbone

Low ringbone, another cause of lameness that can be diagnosed by X-rays, is bone formation in the area of the joint between the coffin bone and the next bone above, the second phalanx. It causes chronic lameness that is difficult to treat or control. **X-rays can also be used to differentiate between low ringbone and high ringbone.** High ringbone is the deposition of bone higher up on the second phalanx. It may cause a visible bulge on the phalanx but is not associated with any serious lameness problems.

Splints

Splint-bone problems are usually so obvious from the outside there is not much point in doing an X-ray for a diagnosis. X-rays are helpful, however, if the splint inflammation is in an unusual location or if there is any reason to suspect a fracture of the splint bone. X-rays may also be helpful with high splint-bone problems, which occur at the top of the splint bone, under the bones of the knee. Inflammation here will appear as a fuzziness to the outlines of the bone, probably with corresponding changes seen on the lower row of knee bones.

High splints may cause no obvious outward signs of swelling or heat because they are located under a dense and tight layer of connective tissue. High-splint problems can be at the root of difficult-to-explain front-leg soreness, which often has an on-again, off-again pattern.

Knee problems

Arthritis of the knees is most often a problem in horses that race but can occur in horses with poor conformation. X-rays will show the expected osteophyte formation if arthritis is a problem. You may also be able to see changes in the joint space — the area between the bones in the joint that is filled with fluid. Joint-space changes, specifically narrowing, indicate either insufficient joint fluid or a poor alignment of the bones — either one an indicator that problems could occur or are already present.

However, with knee arthritis, there is less certainty that the changes seen really are the cause of the horse's present pain (similar to the situation in hocks). **Many horses get by quite well despite having extensive X-ray changes, as long as they are not worked too heavily or too fast.** Nerve/joint blocks are usually indicated to confirm knee pain, even in the presence of positive X-rays.

Hock problems

Hocks are unique in that once arthritis starts in the lower hock joint, it will often progress to a state where the osteophytes actually form "bridges" between the bones and prevent them from moving. **This causes dramatic changes on X-rays, but "fused" hock joints are usually quite pain-free.**

Before fusion is complete, however, horses often experience problems with varying levels of lameness. About the only way to be totally sure a present problem is coming from this area is to use local anesthesia. Commonly used tests, such as holding the hock up in a flexed position and jogging the horse off after this, are of little use since partially

A clinical examination is usually necessary along with X-rays in determining the cause and severity of lameness problems.

fused hocks may not be a problem for the horse that is used lightly, but the flexion test itself will cause pain.

However, some horses never actually achieve a full fusion of the bones and are plagued by chronic (although sometimes mild) stiffness in their hocks. Other horses may appear to have fused bones but remain lame for unclear reasons (either the fusion is not as complete as it looks or there are changes to the cartilage of the hock that are invisible on X-rays but painful nevertheless).

Osteochondrosis dessicans

Osteochondrosis (OCD) is a disease of the cartilage lining of joints. It probably has its origin in the nutrition of the pregnant mare and young horse but may not appear as a lameness until later in life, when the horse is put into work. OCD can involve virtually any joint and commonly will be found in more than one location, with or without a history of the horse ever having lameness problems there.

OCD is difficult to diagnose on X-rays, especially using portable equipment with limited options for improving the quality of the X-ray. OCD causes cracking, thinning and flap-forming in the cartilage. Other changes include cysts inside the bone in the region immediately adjacent to the cartilage and fracturing off of small pieces of bone and cartilage (called "joint mice"). These pieces float around in the joint and may cause irritation if they are pinched between bones as the joint moves.

Of all the possible changes to the joint with OCD, joint mice are the easiest to pick up on X-rays. Cracks and flaps of cartilage are usually not visible on standard X-rays. Areas where cartilage is completely thinned out can sometimes be seen as a dip in the outline of the bone, surrounded by a small, more dense rim of bone that forms as a reaction to the inflammation. However, this is a subtle finding and will usually not be evident to anyone other than a radiologist.

Similarly, bone cysts can be difficult to pick up on regular X-rays. If OCD is suspected, the veterinarian may refer the horse to a university or large clinic for special tests. One such test is called Xeroradiography. This is a special technique that produces blue-and-white prints instead of the more familiar black-and-white X-ray negatives. It shows much greater detail in the bone and joint surfaces and can also pick up soft-tissue structures, such as tendons and ligaments.

Putting X-rays to work

Let's take the example of a barrel-racing horse who experienced a severe sliding problem when rounding a barrel in a competition about a month ago. This horse has been lame or sore ever since but does not show much swelling anywhere in the legs and is not carrying a lot of "heat" (surface area does not feel warm).

X-rays of the horse's hocks look normal. Does this mean the hocks are not the cause of his lameness? No. The X-rays tell you that the horse does not have a longstanding problem with arthritis. To utilize X-rays in determining if a recent injury is the cause of this horse's problem, you would wait another two weeks or so to see if any changes show up.

A more reliable approach would be to have the veterinarian do a series of nerve blocks and joint blocks to determine where the pain is in the leg. (It could be any of the joints of the lower leg, the pelvis, the back or any of the "soft" tissues that were pulled, strained, sprained, torn or otherwise stressed.)

Staying with the hocks as an example, let's look at the flip side of the coin. Another patient is a 15-year-old pleasure horse who does not have a particularly strenuous work schedule but does have times when he is used heavily. It's the end of spring, and he's just completed an extensive overnight trail ride. Two days after returning home, the horse is noticeably stiff and sore behind.

The veterinarian takes hock X-rays, which show typical osteophyte formation. Are these osteophytes the source of this horse's pain? Maybe — or maybe not.

In a horse this age, radiographic evidence of arthritis is not unusual. Those osteophytes could have formed years before, from a problem that may no longer bother the horse. However, their presence does raise suspicion that the hocks could be causing the lameness, since they do at least tell you the horse has had hock problems in the past.

To be more certain the problem is the hocks, you would have to compare the current X-rays with X-rays taken at least several months earlier that do not show osteophytes, or show that they were smaller than they are now. Even then, an accurate diagnosis will require flexion tests, nerve blocks and additional evaluation.

Predicting the future with X-rays

Horseowners often expect X-rays to tell them what the horse's soundness will be in the future, but this is nearly impossible to do. Sometimes, as we've described, X-rays don't even tell if a horse's present problem is related to the findings, or lack of findings.

X-rays point out irregularities that may not be currently causing a problem but are likely to create difficulties later, such as a bone chip. **If you are considering the purchase of a horse that will involve a considerable investment of time, emotions, training or money, having X-rays taken is a good idea both to see what the horse's condition is now; but also, should problems arise, you'll have a basis of X-ray comparison.**

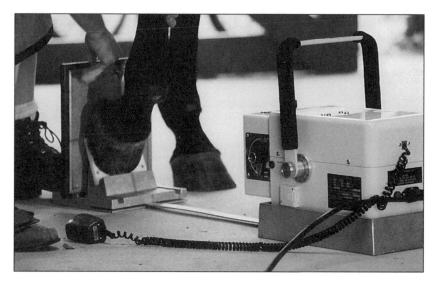

Frequently, it is necessary to take X-rays from various angles in order to get the best diagnosis. Getting the best pictures often requires removal of the horse's shoe.

Too many variables are involved to accurately predict if a horse's X-ray-defined disease will cause future problems. Navicular disease is a good example. There are many young horses who have had definite evidence of navicular disease on their X-rays but who have returned to soundness when shoeing and balancing problems were corrected. With older horses, it is often difficult to draw the line between navicular-bone changes that you would expect to see occur over time and those that reflect an actual degeneration process.

The lesson here is not to be too hard on the veterinarian if he or she seems reluctant to give you any hard answers. X-rays are only one piece of information you need to consider when making a decision about a horse's future soundness. The type of work he will be doing, the individual horse's tolerance for discomfort, the availability of medication or other therapy to help the horse and the presence or absence of contributing factors you can correct (i.e., shoeing, footing) all play a role. ■PH■

Section II

Veterinary Care
For The Horse
With Health Problems

7

Coping With Arthritis

*Keeping a horse with arthritis comfortable
requires detecting changes in his level of pain and
knowing how to deal with chronic pain and flare-ups.*

As anyone with arthritis can tell you, joint pain is a daily problem. While researchers work to develop treatments that can greatly alleviate or even eventually cure arthritis, for the time being it must be considered a chronic degenerative disease. Basically, what this means is that arthritis will always be present and, left unchecked, will progress on a gradual downhill course. Keeping an arthritic horse comfortable need not be a hopeless task but will require constant attention.

Arthritis is the degeneration of a joint. From a nutritional standpoint, it can result when there are inadequate amounts of the nutrients essential to form the joint (developmental joint disease), to control the damaging effects of exercise or trauma and/or to keep up with the demand of repairing and maintaining a joint. Arthritis involves:

- Cartilage — the smooth lining over the ends of bones that permits them to glide easily over each other.
- Synovium — the tissue located along the inside of joints, which produces joint fluid.
- Bones, which can be irritated to the point of producing excessive layers of bone and forming "spurs" or points of bone along their edges.
- Ligaments inside a joint.
- The tough outer capsule of joints that helps to stabilize the joint structure and holds in the joint fluid.

Lying down more fre- quently than usual is often a sign of arthritis pain.

Arthritis can be initiated by problems related to trauma or poor conformation or may arise in a horse's later years as a result of the cumulative effect of wear and tear on the joint. Arthritis may also have its roots in improper development of joints in the fetus or young horse (developmental bone disease, such as OCD — osteochondrosis dessicans).

Arthritis often begins as an inflammation, commonly of the synovium, joint capsule or tendons and ligaments of a joint. If inflammation is not controlled, it will affect the quality of the joint fluid. **Joint fluid is the only source of nutrition for the cartilage in a joint, as cartilage does not normally have any blood supply.** When nutrition to the joint is disrupted by interference with the production of normal joint fluid, cartilage weakens and becomes worn. Inadequate cartilage and abnormal joint fluid greatly decrease the ability of a joint to withstand loading and compression. When this happens, movement becomes painful. If the situation is not corrected, further degeneration occurs and the arthritis becomes progressively worse.

Our understanding of arthritis and other joint problems is still incomplete. However, we know from research that we can greatly influence the course of arthritis through proper nutrition, and there are measures we can take to help our horses be more comfortable. Beyond that, the better you know and observe your horse, the better you'll be able to recognize when he's feeling pretty good and when he's having a hard day.

Once you become sensitive to your horse's way of showing pain, you can make adjustments in his level of work and the treatment you give. **Occasional bad days are often associated with cold, damp weather and not getting the usual amount of turnout.**

If the horse is having an obvious escalation in symptoms, usually caused by more than the accustomed level of work but sometimes without a clear cause, he should be treated for an acute arthritis flare-up.

Signs of arthritic pain

Most people can spot a horse who is obviously lame, even if they cannot immediately pinpoint which joint or even which leg is bothering him. However, the signs of joint pain may be subtle and may include:

■ *A subdued or depressed attitude. A variation on this is a horse who becomes sullen or "sour," especially about work.*

■ *Decreased appetite.*

■ *Lying down more often than usual.*

■ *When turned out, the horse will likely not move around as much or as quickly as usual and be less interested in play.*

■ *The horse may isolate himself from companions.*

■ *When in the stall, a horse with joint pain will usually find a way to ease the weight to the involved leg. With a front leg, this usually means keeping the leg farther out in front of him, rather than directly under his body.*

■ *When you pick his feet, you will notice that the foot on the "bad" leg has less straw, manure and dirt packed into it.*

■ *Horses with a sore hind leg will either keep it flexed, taking the weight on the "good" (or better) side, or will place it in an abnormal position, usually farther in front and/or more under the body than normal.*

■ *When being ridden, a horse with arthritis pain will usually seem to be "stiff." Stride length may be short- ened, and he will resist turning toward the affected leg.*

> ■ *Anything that increases strain on the painful leg (i.e., faster gait, turn on the haunches, turn on the forehand, lateral work, jumping, collected work) will be performed poorly or with obvious resistance or refusal. Many serious behavioral problems, such as rearing and barn sourness, have their roots in joint pain. Horses in pain may also "blow" or breathe harder than you would expect for the level of work they are doing.*

Keep him comfortable

While cold is a formidable weapon in fighting arthritis flare-ups, heat is the friend of the chronically arthritic joint. Familiar human remedies, such as Ben-Gay and Icy Hot, work on the principle that creating a mild inflammation in the area of an arthritic joint increases blood flow, improves flexibility and makes the area less painful. The same holds true for horses, with Absorbine being the best-known liniment.

Bandaging, which is really only effective or practical for the ankle, can help protect a joint from excessive or jerking movements. However, bandaging also helps to hold in heat, which is beneficial in all arthritic joints. Even standard stall bandages can accomplish this to some extent.

More effective is the use of Neoprene wraps or sweats, which fasten with hook-and-loop closures and adjust to various sizes of joints. Neoprene sweats are most often used on the hocks and knees. You can achieve the same effect in other areas by using a layer of plastic wrap either alone or over cotton stall bandages.

In addition to providing heat, bandaging helps control swelling. The pressure of a bandage prevents excessive amounts of fluid from accumulating. When bandages are Neoprene or you use

Hydrotherapy — using either warm or cold water, depending on the situation — is a time-honored, effective treatment.

plastic wrap, you get the added benefit of local fluid loss by "sweat-ing." You can even heat and "sweat" arthritic backs by using a show-er curtain liner or plastic tablecloth under a sheet or blanket.

Liniments, rubs and braces increase the heating effect of ban-dages. The biggest challenge is often to find one that does not cause too much skin irritation. Menthol-based rubs are usually the least irritating (these provide surface cool sensation but deeper heating). Use of a liniment with a witch-hazel base instead of alcohol is also easier on the skin.

Experiment with several products until you find one that does not cause skin flaking (called "scurf") and that the horse enjoys. He will get the most benefit if you spend 10 minutes or so massaging or rubbing the leg briskly with the liniment before applying his ban-dages. (Note: Some liniments are too irritating to be used under Neo-prene or plastic sweats. Read instructions carefully, and use caution if you know your horse has sensitive skin.) It is important to avoid skin irritation, if possible, since this will often be painful enough to interfere with an adequate assessment of how much pain is com-ing from the joint itself.

DMSO

DMSO deserves special consideration because of its unique proper-ties. **DMSO can break up fluid collections so that they are more eas-ily removed by the body.** DMSO also has direct anti-inflammatory properties of its own. It penetrates through the skin quite easily and can be used to carry low doses of medications, such as corticosteroids, into the joint, greatly reducing the chances of side effects.

Although DMSO does not have any known harmful side effects in horses, it is potentially damaging to human eyes with long-term exposure. Always wear gloves when applying DMSO.

DMSO has a strong offensive odor, said by some to be like garlic, people also report a strange taste in their mouth after DMSO being absorbed into their skin anywhere on their body.

Presumably horses also find the same thing, as many will object to being rubbed with DMSO after enough has been absorbed for them to taste it. There may also be a mild local irritation, but this is obvi-ously hard to determine since the horse can't tell us what he does not like. If you try DMSO, be forewarned: The horse may not like it.

DMSO is also more likely to cause flaking of the skin, especial-ly if applied under a bandage. In mild cases, this is only due to de-hydration of the surface layers of skin. However, if the underlying

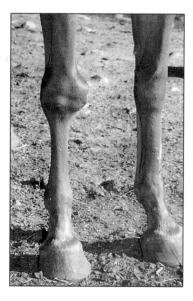

This mare's arthritic knee is the result of an injury as a two-year-old, which obviously prevented her from having a career as a performance horse. Fortunately, she's well-bred enough to serve as a broodmare.

joint has a significant amount of inflammation, the skin reaction can be more severe and make the horse uncomfortable, although it is not actually harmful. If you run into problems when using DMSO, ask for your veterinarian's advice.

Shoeing

Shoeing cannot cure arthritis, but it can make movement mechanically easier. Squaring the toes (front and/or rear hooves) makes breakover easier and smoother. Keep the feet at a natural angle in front to avoid forcing the bones into an unnatural alignment. Avoid all grabs, caulks or trailers on the shoe. A horse with arthritic hocks or stifles will often benefit from raising the angle of the rear hooves to at least 54° to 56°. Special degree pads are available for both the front and back feet. Using these pads, the farrier can achieve the desired angles immediately, without having to wait for the heels to grow.

Magnetic therapy

There is growing evidence that magnetic therapy may benefit horses with arthritis. You can purchase boots, wraps and even blankets that contain magnets. The magnets work, at least in part, by improving blood flow. Studies have shown that this effect is more than skin deep — underlying bones and joints have improved blood flow. Improved blood flow means improved metabolism of the cells, improved delivery of nutrients and improved removal of waste products. However, magnetic equipment is fairly expensive and may not offer much more relief than methods of applying heat, such as massage, liniments, hot-water therapy, bandaging and so forth. Before spending the money for magnetic therapy equipment, arrange to borrow a unit to see if it will actually help your horse.

Exercising the horse with arthritis

*While heavy exercise is often one of the initiating events in arthritis, lack of exercise is deadly to arthritic joints. **If joints are not kept moving, permanent restriction of motion may result.** Tissues surrounding the joint become weaker, thinner and shortened, resulting in what is termed a "contracture." This limits the mobility of the joint, and any attempts to move it normally are painful. If the joint is actively producing extra bone at its edges, or if bone is exposed under areas of cartilage loss, the bones can even grow together to form a "fusion," which permanently limits the movement of the joint. Gentle exercise on a daily basis may prevent this from happening.*

*Exercise is also important to the overall health of the joint. **Multiple studies have shown that exercise improves the quality of joint fluid and stimulates metabolism in the joint.** After injury or insult to a joint in an experimental situation, animals that are lightly exercised recover far more quickly and completely than those that are only rested. In horses, resumption of light, regular exercise can improve the outcome when medications are injected into a joint. Exercise can even prevent the negative side effects of corticosteroid injection into a joint.*

*Common sense is the key. **Exercise must be regular but not excessive**. Walking without stopping for 20 to 30 minutes a day or gentle trotting, if the degree of lameness permits, is sufficient. Keeping the horse turned out as much as possible helps the horse overall, but it is not enough exercise to help the joint. In addition to exercise, simply picking up the horse's leg and moving the joint through flexion and extension (i.e., for a knee, flex the leg as far as it will go, then extend it) 10 to 15 times, several times a day or whenever you think of it, will also help keep that important flexibility.*

Arthritis flare-ups

Arthritis flare-ups are, precipitated by an injury, overwork, a simple bad step or even for reasons you cannot pinpoint. When this happens, quick action will restore the horse to a comfortable state and minimize the chances of a joint being damaged further.

This is one time where "quick-fix" drugs may be indicated for a short time — one or two doses at most. Phenylbutazone orally or by injection can be used, as can any anti-inflammatory that your veterinarian recommends.

There are also many things you can do for the horse to help him get comfortable. **Icing the joint and cold-water therapy provide more than relief. They work directly to control the inflammation and swelling — the most important concern with acute arthritis flares.**

Cold decreases blood flow, slowing delivery of inflammatory cells and chemicals. Cold also slows down any inflammatory processes that are already underway and reduces or eliminates swelling. **The newest work on postsurgical management of orthopedic (bone and joint) cases shows that constant application of cold during the 24 to 48 hours postoperatively improves pain relief, speeds healing and hastens recovery.** Standing a foundered horse in a running stream is an old, effective treatment that shows the power of cold therapy.

The acutely arthritic horse should be kept in a well-bedded stall or small paddock with deep footing for the first 24 to 48 hours — until the acute inflammation is under control. Forced exercise is not advisable. However, you can gently put the joint through flexion and extension several times a day to keep it from feeling stiff — or, ultimately, from actually becoming stiff.

While bandaging can be helpful in controlling swelling, it is likely to cause the area to hold too much heat — the opposite of what you want to happen when the horse is in this acute state.

The exception is in the case of a fetlock joint. The ankle is put under a tremendous strain even when the horse is standing still, since the ankle is designed to have a wide range of movement and acts as a shock absorber. A light bandage with support under the ankle, or a manufactured therapeutic boot with ankle support, will relieve the strain on this joint when it is inflamed.

Nutritionally, you should increase the dosage of antioxidant vitamins during an arthritis flare-up. Short-term use of vitamin C at seven grams or more, increased bioflavinoids and vitamin E in 2,000 to 5,000 IU dosages is quite safe and will help bring the inflammation

It is not uncommon to find older show horses with arthritic ankles.

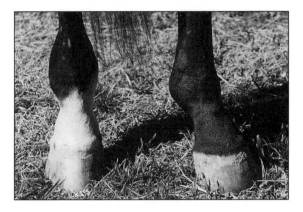

under control. Increasing any joint supplements you are feeding (glucosamine, etc.) to full recommended dose or even more will also help minimize any joint damage.

Once the horse is more comfortable (usually within 48 to 72 hours), you can cut back on the cold therapy and begin hand walking for 10 to 15 minutes several times a day. Make sure this amount of time is actually spent walking — not walking over to the nearest patch of grass and grazing. If the horse tolerates this well, gradually ease him back onto his regular exercise program and amount of turnout.

NOTE: If the horse is not obviously improved in 48 to 72 hours, or if he cannot seem to tolerate his old level of exercise, even introduced gradually, consult your veterinarian. There may be a new injury to the area that will require adjustments in your treatment plan.

Allergies and arthritis

Many doctors strongly suspect that food allergies are at the root of many causes of arthritis in people. We know virtually nothing about this possibility in horses. If your horse shows any other signs of being an allergy-prone individual (i.e., stable cough or "heaves," frequent skin problems, "feed bumps," itching, prone to digestive upsets), you may want to try eliminating potential offending materials from his diet to see if this helps. Corn and soybean products (often added to sweet feeds or pellets to boost the total protein content) are the most likely offenders. Yeast, wheat bran and rice bran should also be avoided, as well as feeds containing brewer's grains. Wait at least six weeks after eliminating a type of feed or feed additive to decide if eliminating that element of the horse's diet made any change in his arthritis.

Feeding arthritic horses

Maximizing nutrition should be one of the primary goals in any treatment. In the case of arthritis, the approach is double pronged. You must keep the horse at an appropriate weight but guarantee he receives a generous amount of all the different nutrients he needs to build healthy joints and supply the nutritional factors needed to keep inflammation from getting out of hand.

All the important internal structures of a joint — the cartilage, joint capsule, synovium and ligaments — are connective tissue. Connective tissue is composed in large part of collagen, a substance made up of simple sugars, proteins and minerals. Simple carbohydrates (sugars) are in adequate supply in virtually any equine diet. The protein needed is a different story.

Meeting a horse's overall total protein needs (i.e., percent of protein in the diet) is not difficult to do using common grains and hays. However, it must be the right kind of protein. The arthritic horse must receive adequate amounts of lysine in his protein source. **Lysine, an amino acid essential to proper growth and tissue repair, allows the animal to utilize his other amino acids more efficiently.**

The horse will also need adequate amounts of the special sulfur-containing amino acids, such as methionine and cystine. Many, if not most, diets commonly fed to horses are borderline-to-deficient in these amino acids, even for maintenance or light work. If you add the job of repairing and maintaining joints, demand can easily exceed supply.

When speaking about mineral requirements and joints, recent studies have linked both low copper and low zinc intakes to increased risk of foals being born with abnormal joint cartilage (developmental joint disease). Manganese is another element critical to joints.

There are various enzyme systems within joints and throughout the entire body whose function is to control inflammation. One of the major anti-inflammatory enzymes is superoxide dismutase (SOD). This enzyme neutralizes free radicals — electrically charged molecules generated by the inflammatory process as well as by exercise — that will damage nearby normal tissues as they search for an opposite electrical charge to neutralize them. SOD is in abundant supply. However, the catch is that it cannot work without the proper levels of key trace minerals: zinc, copper, selenium and magnesium. Not surprisingly, these minerals are also nutrients that are likely to be in short supply, if not deficient, in many common diets.

Last, but far from least important, are the antioxidant vitamins. Antioxidant vitamins also combat free radicals, snatching them up and neutralizing them before they can damage nearby tissues.

In the case of joints, vitamins E and C most important. Both can neutralize free radicals. Vitamin C is also capable of taking free radicals from vitamin E, thus reactivating the vitamin E, and it is essential to the normal formation of collagen. Another class of antioxidants, the bioflavinoids, are found in the peel of citrus fruits. They make vitamin C work more efficiently. There are many more antioxidant substances that scientists have identified and more will probably appear in time. These include lipoic acid, coenzyme Q-10 and proanthocyanins (isolated from pine bark and grape seeds).

Having now identified the major nutrients needed to control arthritis and help joints repair themselves, the next step is to meet those needs.

Building the diet

Beginning with protein, unless you are feeding alfalfa hay, you will come up short on lysine. Methionine levels are difficult to gauge in equine diets and (as with all the amino acids) likely to be variable, depending on the quality of the hay or grain. Further compounding the problem is that we really do not know exactly how much a horse needs. Manna Pro's Calf Manna or Amino-Fac from Uckele Animal Health are both good choices as protein supplements. Feed about 1/2 pound per day for maintenance, more with heavy work. How-

ever, you will not need a protein supplement if you are feeding high-quality alfalfa at or above maintenance levels (one percent of body weight per day).

Mineral supplementation is advisable for all horses with arthritis, regardless of diet. Requirements for manganese, copper, zinc and selenium can all be reasonably expected to be higher. If the horse is being worked, requirements will be higher yet. Opt-E-Horse by Weaver Leather is an excellent source of all the key minerals and also provides some vitamin E. The relatively low selenium content of this product makes it safe to feed in all locations. However, if you live in a low-selenium area, additional selenium may be needed. If you choose Opt-E-Horse, supplement this with a vitamin C product (such as Select-Pet's Ester C or Vita-Flex Pure C), plain vitamin E (1,000 IU per day without work, and up to 3,000 IU or more with work) in high-selenium areas or a vitamin E-and-selenium supplement in low-selenium areas.

While not a complete vitamin and mineral supplement, Vita-Key's Antioxidant Concentrate provides what you need for supplementing a horse with arthritis: the correct amount of trace minerals, antioxidant vitamins, lysine and methionine. If you are already using a supplement for reasons beyond arthritis, check with your veterinarian about what your horse may need, so you don't double up on vitamins or minerals the horse doesn't need and further complicate his situation. ▣

8

Understanding Colic

*Colic. The very word makes most
horsepeople nervous — and with good reason.
But what exactly causes it, and
how can you help your horse?*

C olic is a broad term that means the horse has pain in his abdomen. It has many possible causes, some more serious than others. Before a discussion of the different types of colic, one thing needs to be made clear: **Colic should always be considered a medical emergency. The early stages of a potentially fatal colic appear no different from those of a less-serious abdominal problem.** Only a veterinarian can determine how serious the colic really is.

CAUSES OF COLIC
Bloodworms

Parasites (worms) are a common cause of colic, although the use of modern worming drugs, such as ivermectin, has greatly reduced this problem. Most people associate poor weight gain, rough hair coat and "pot belly" with parasites. Worms can cause some of these difficulties, but there are others symptoms, including colic.

On one level, parasites compete with the horse for food, but they also damage the intestinal tract by attacking and invading the lining of the intestines and sometimes traveling even farther in the body. As adults, the parasites *Strongylus vulgaris* — the so-called "bloodworms" — live inside the lumen (the hollow center of the tube of

Horses often lie down or roll in an attempt to relieve abdominal pain. If the horse is lying quietly, let him rest, but try to get him back up on his feet if he attempts to roll.

the intestine, where foods and fluids pass), quietly sharing the food supply and laying eggs. However, the "baby" worms invade the wall of the intestine and travel extensively throughout the arteries that supply the intestine with blood.

The photo on page 84 shows a section of a horse's small intestine — the section that comes just after the stomach. The normally smooth, pink surface is covered by raised, darkened areas that resemble blood blisters. This is damage caused by the immature forms of the strongyle parasite.

They can even travel up along the major arteries to the intestine near the aorta, causing clots to form. **Even relatively minor bloodworm damage can result in a section of intestine receiving an inadequate blood supply, causing it to lose its ability to function and eventually to die.**

Inadequate blood supply is called "ischemia" and causes the horse pain, which worsens when there is food in the intestine and more blood is needed to perform the functions of digestion.

Once damage to the intestines from bloodworms has occurred, it may be irreversible. Many horses with recurrent bouts of colic throughout their lives are suffering from the permanent effects of worm damage.

Other parasites

A typical protozoan found in a horse's large intestines. The protozoan does the work of digesting fibrous material.

Many other types of intestinal parasites can affect horses. Some cause irritation or damage to the lining of the intestine, which interferes with absorption of food and causes the horse to lose fluids, electrolytes and proteins into the intestinal tract. Damaged intestinal linings also make the horse more susceptible to absorbing dangerous bacteria or toxins into his bloodstream.

Some parasites invade the wall of the intestine and damage blood or nerve supplies, potentially causing that section of the bowel to become damaged and unable to contract normally to pass food along. The common roundworm, which can be found in virtually every foal and often plagues horses in the older years as well, damages not only the intestine but also migrates through the liver and lungs, causing damage in these organs and increasing the likelihood of infections.

The longer parasites remain unchecked, the greater the damage will be — easily progressing to the point that the horse will have problems with colic to some degree throughout his life. This is one form of colic you can prevent by following rigorous deworming schedules as recommended by your veterinarian. **An investment of about $100 per year in deworming drugs may save you thousands in emergency veterinary colic treatment.**

Strongylus edentatus parasite.

Indigestion and overeating

Indigestion/overeating to us is that uncomfortable, full feeling in the stomach/upper abdomen. The same problem can occur when horses either eat too much at one time or when they eat too quickly, especially if water is not taken in to help move things along.

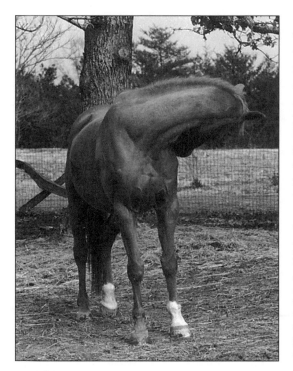

Horses with abdominal pain turn around often to look at their sides.

The unique structure of the horse's throat prevents gas, food or fluid from coming up from the stomach. **Therefore, problems that could be relieved in people simply by belching or, if necessary, vomiting, will persist and worsen in the horse.** Horses with this type of abdominal pain show signs of mild-to-moderate discomfort. They will pass manure normally (since that portion of the digestive tract is not involved) but will paw, stretch out and prefer to lie down — some insist on lying down. Once down, they may lie quietly or appear restless. They may roll if pain is of sufficient intensity.

To relieve this type of abdominal pain, a tube must be passed into the horse's nostril, through his throat and down into the stomach. **This is a fairly tricky procedure, a job for your veterinarian only, as entering the wrong opening and going into the horse's lungs could have serious, even fatal, consequences.**

Once the stomach tube has been successfully passed, relief will be rapid. The veterinarian will often then pass water or both water and mineral oil through the tube to help move things along.

A different type of indigestion can occur in horses if too much protein or concentrated carbohydrate (grain) is eaten and not properly digested in the stomach and small intestine before it reaches the horse's large intestine (the cecum and colon).

The large intestine has a sizable population of various bacteria and organisms called protozoa, as well as yeasts. These "bugs" do the work of digesting food that people and animals with simpler intestinal tracts cannot digest — the more fibrous plant materials in grasses and hays.

If "richer" foods such as proteins and grains reach this area of the intestine, they will also be digested by the organisms, but will produce greater-than-normal amounts of gas and byproducts, such as lactic acid.

These byproducts can then kill those organisms normally present to digest the complex plant materials. This results in imbalances of the organisms and the absorption of potentially toxic byproducts into the horse's blood stream.

Unfortunately, these richer foods tend to feed species of bacteria that produce dangerous toxins. As they flourish, the beneficial populations are wiped out, the intestine becomes irritated, acidity builds up and gas accumulates. The intestine becomes sluggish and distended from gas. Intestinal pain results. **In extreme cases, like overeating grain, the horse may absorb enough of the toxins to produce other complications, such as laminitis (founder).**

Because the intestine is not moving normally, fluid will also build up (the intestine normally secretes large amounts of fluid into the lumen) and back up, sometimes as far as the stomach. Initial treatment consists of passing a stomach tube to relieve gas or fluid backup, administration of fluid and mineral oil, and possibly pain medications. The veterinarian may give an antacid such as sodium bicarbonate either by stomach tube or into the horse's vein.

Horses whose mouth membranes are red or blue are probably in a toxic situation and may require additional medications and intravenous fluids. Other intestinal complications, such as obstruction or twisting, can occur, especially if treatment is delayed.

Obstructions to the flow of food

If the flow of fluids and solids along the intestinal tract becomes partially or completely blocked, the ingesta (material the horse has taken in) becomes firmly packed, while gas and fluid accumulate and back up. You may see small amounts of diarrhea even though the horse is constipated, because fluids and gases often get past the blockage. Passage of small amounts of stool covered by mucus is also common.

Obstructions may be mechanical, such as sand, tumor or a fecolith (an intestinal stone), or caused by the twisting, kinking or telescoping of the bowel. Symptoms depend on both the duration and

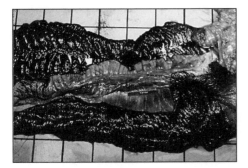

Once damage to the intestines from bloodworms has occurred, it may be irreversible. The dark area is dead tissue; the lighter color shows the healthy section.

the degree of the obstruction. Early cases with some material getting through will have less-severe symptoms.

Mechanical obstructions often require surgery, while impactions of food material only may respond to the treatment as other colics (stomach tube, mineral oil and medication) but could require several days of treatment before being resolved. Common causes of non-mechanical obstruction include decreased water intake and/or decreased availability of drinkable water and abnormal movement of a section of intestine caused by previous parasite damage.

Twists and related problems

The intestinal tract of the horse is large and long. Much of it lies inside the abdomen covered by a layer of tissue called the omentum, but it is not directly attached to the wall of the abdomen or other structures.

It is suspended from a sheet of tissue called the mesentery, containing the arteries and veins that supply the intestine. It originates along the top/roof of the abdomen (under the backbone), in the region of the aorta, the major artery of the body. The intestine can move about in the abdomen, but under normal circumstances the various parts will stay in pretty much the same position.

However, if the intestine becomes distended with gas or fluid, or heavily weighed down by backed-up ingesta, it may move about in unusual ways and become kinked, twisted on itself or twisted by spinning around its mesentery. A similar type of problem is called intussusception and occurs when a section of intestine folds inside itself, like the sections of a telescope when you close it.

It is possible for a horse to cause one of the above problems by rolling too vigorously. However, this is unlikely to occur unless there is already another intestinal problem causing a backup of fluid, gas or solids. Therefore, these problems may actually be complications of any one of the other types of colic described earlier. Often, the initial cause is never determined.

Twists and similar problems are serious because they commonly involve a shutoff of blood supply to the involved section of intestine and are associated with blockage of flow along the bowel. Death/destruction of the involved segment can occur, releasing bacteria and toxins into both the blood stream (causing toxemia) and the abdominal cavity (causing an inflammation called peritonitis), in which case the horse's life is in danger.

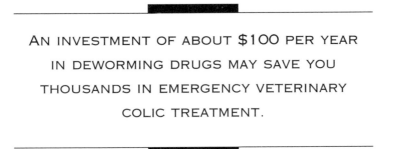

AN INVESTMENT OF ABOUT $100 PER YEAR IN DEWORMING DRUGS MAY SAVE YOU THOUSANDS IN EMERGENCY VETERINARY COLIC TREATMENT.

Signs or symptoms of such a severe colic include severe pain, very abnormal pulse, respiration and possibly temperature, red-to-blue/gray mucus membranes (in late stages) and all the behavior changes associated with the severe pain (agitation, desire to roll, heavy sweating and refusal to stand).

However, the horse will usually not quickly go from completely normal into this very-ill state. The observant owner/trainer will pick up the early signs and, by calling the vet immediately, may be able to get help for the horse before it is too late.

Treatment on the farm will include the same measures we have talked about before (stomach tube, pain medications, etc.). A major difference in these cases is that the rectal examination will eventually reveal findings of distended loops of intestine that signal a serious problem. By combining the rectal examination findings with information on the horse's other signs and symptoms, especially a pattern of worsening and poor response to pain medications, the veterinarian will be able to decide when and if the horse needs to have surgery.

Stress-related causes

Horses in high-stress situations, such as unaccustomed or prolonged exercise (like the first day of training) or prolonged shipping, may show the same signs as a horse with mild colic. This could be due to decreased intestinal motility, dehydration, an "indigestion" or maybe a pain that mimics colic (i.e., muscular). In any case, these horses warrant the same close observation and evaluation.

What to do if your horse colics

The caretaker can often mean the difference between life and death for the horse. Your first job is to be observant. If the horse shows any signs of a possible abdominal problem, investigate.

A drop in appetite is often the first sign of intestinal trouble. Check the stall for other clues, such as a change in, or absence of, manure. Note the horse's general attitude, and take his pulse, temperature and respiration. Check the color of the mucus membranes. Write down all the information and call the veterinarian for advice.

NOTE: Never give pain medications to the horse unless specifically instructed to do so by the veterinarian. Medication may mask symptoms.

If the horse seems uncomfortable and wants to roll, take him outside to a grassy area and walk him. Walking will help take the horse's mind off the pain and also help improve the movement of gas, fluid and solids along the intestine. If the weather permits, hosing the horse with warm water may also be a soothing distraction. It is wise to restrict walking to grassy areas, in the event the horse insists on going down.

When the veterinarian arrives

On arrival, the veterinarian will ask about the horse and the problem. This is where your written notes provide valuable information. The veterinarian will then check the horse's pulse, respiration and temperature, as well as the color of the mucus membranes. An examination of the chest and abdomen is done with a stethoscope to pick up any abnormal sounds.

The veterinarian will usually pass a stomach tube to determine if there is a backup of gas or fluids and to relieve the pressure. (This makes many horses more comfortable so that they are easier to examine.)

A rectal examination is also normally done. The veterinarian will put on a long plastic glove and reach into the rectum. Distended sections of intestine can be felt through the wall of the rectum (they feel like water balloons). It is also sometimes possible to feel tight bands of tissue if the intestine is twisted or otherwise out of position.

The veterinarian will then treat the horse and inform you of what the next step should be. NOTE: The order in which these things are done may change depending on the circumstances. For example, a horse that is agitated and appears to be having a great deal of pain may require pain medication and passage of the stomach tube before a complete examination.

Signs and Symptoms of Abdominal Pain

- **Depression** *(early), agitation (late, serious sign).*

- **Change in appetite** — *usually refusal of grain before refusing hay (early sign), to complete loss of appetite.*

- **Decreased water consumption** — *the horse may splash around without drinking.*

- **Sweating** — *usually moderate-to-severe pain.*

- **Laying down** — *the horse will often lie quietly if pain is mild.*

- **Turning to look at the belly.**

- **Pawing.**

- **Tail elevated** *with or without passage of gas.*

- **Kicking at the belly.**

- **Rolling** *moderate-to-severe pain.*

■ **Change in color of the mucus membranes** (lining) of
the lips and gums:
  — Pale pink — normal
  — Very white — shock or bleeding
  — Red — toxins in the blood, serious sign
  — Bluish purple/gray — shock and toxins in blood,
    very serious sign

■ **Standing stretched out** as if attempting to urinate

■ **A change in manure** may precede signs of pain:
  — Less manure than normal
  — Drier manure than normal
  — Mucus coating manure (may be in thick "threads")
  — Diarrhea

■ **Elevated respiratory rate** (breaths per minute) will
increase in proportion to the amount of pain.

■ **Elevated pulse rate** (heart beats per minute) will
increase in proportion to the amount of pain.

Sample colic information sheet

Set up a sheet to make recording all the important information
organized and easy. You will then have a good record of symptoms
to show the veterinarian when he/she arrives. One of the most
important tools the veterinarian uses in deciding whether a colic is
serious enough to require transport to a hospital and possible surgery
is knowing the severity of the symptoms and the pattern they show
(severe and rapidly worsening symptoms not helped much by treatment may mean a need for surgery). The more detailed history you
can give the veterinarian, the more useful it will be.

Date: 1-1-99   **Time**: 4:00 P.M.
Pulse: 60   **Respiration**: 20   **Temperature**: 99.8
Symptoms: Did not eat, lying down, mucus
Comments: Very little manure in stall.
          Membranes are pink. ▣

9

Treating Eye Problems

Any injury to the eye, sign of eye pain or
suspected change in vision is an emergency situation:
Eye problems are far more likely
to rapidly get worse than better on their own.

Major symptoms of common eye problems include swelling of the eyelids and surrounding structures, excessive tearing, avoidance of light and excessive redness of the conjunctiva, the moist pink tissue on the inner surface of the lids.

If your horse has an eye problem, place the horse in a darkened stall and call the veterinarian. If examination will be delayed for more than a few hours, began treatment with an ophthalmic antibiotic ointment or drops. **Do not use an ointment containing corticosteroids (prednisolone acetate, for instance, even opthalmic steroids can worsen corneal damage — use these only with your veterinarian's approval).** If you have it on hand, your veterinarian may recommend flunixin meglumine (Banamine) or phenylbutazone ("bute") for pain control and reduction of swelling.

Deep or extensive injuries may be visible with the naked eye. Corneal injuries more than a few hours old will also have caused a whitening of the cornea. Small injuries may only be visible after the eye is stained with fluroscein, a special dye.

The veterinarian will first confirm that nothing is trapped under either lid (usually the upper), such as a piece of plant material or an insect. To do this, the horse's lids must be turned inside out. Then the vet will check to be certain that the corneal surface has not been scratched or cut (especially important if any foreign matter was found under the lids).

Suggested eye medication
to keep on hand

*Every first-aid supply should contain eye medications.
This is especially important if you live or ride in remote
locations and/or if emergency veterinary attention is difficult to obtain. The following are suggested:*

■ **Antibiotic ointment**
Types: *Various formulas/drugs are available. These
include gentamicin, polymixin, triple antibiotic (a mix of
three drugs), chloramphenicol, tobramycin.*
Uses: *With any injury to the eye or signs of irritation to
the eye — to treat any infection already present or help
prevent infection.*
Comments: *Always use only antibiotic medications
specifically labeled for use in the eye (labeled optic or
ophthalmic). Use of other antibiotics may cause damage
or further irritation.*

■ **Antibiotic and steroid combination ointment**
Types: *Again, various antibiotics may be used, usually in
combination with the corticosteroid prednisolone acetate.*
Uses: *Steroid-containing antibiotic ointments are used
for a variety of problems including conjunctivitis, fly irritation and allergy.*
Comments: *Steroid-containing ointments should never be
used unless a veterinarian has examined the eye and
proven there is no damage to the cornea. Steroids
applied to areas of corneal damage lead to broken areas
becoming larger and deeper and also greatly increase the
likelihood of infection of various types.*

■ **Pupillary dilators, drops or ointment**
Types: *Atropine is the most commonly used drug to
dilate pupils and the one least likely to be associated
with side effects.*
Uses: *It is extremely important to keep the pupil dilated
in any eye that has active inflammation, especially if the
inflammation is known to extend into the deeper structures
of the eye.*

Comments: Side effects are rare but mild colic may occur if atropine must be applied frequently (every 1 to 2 hours).

■ *Miscellaneous supplies*
A small flashlight or examination light ("penlight") is useful when attempting to examine the eyes. A hood with dark plastic goggles also comes in handy in the summertime to keep flies away from an injured eye and helps to block out irritating light.

Fly irritation

Irritation from flies is a common source of eye problems. The eyes may look awful and be irritated, but inflammation is usually limited to the conjunctiva and the area of the tear-duct opening (a small, raised bump located in the inner corner of the eye). Potential complications include a secondary bacterial infection, swelling and blockage of the tear duct, causing tears to overflow onto the face and possible permanent narrowing or scarring of the tear duct.

Once the veterinarian has made a diagnosis and determined no other problem is active, you will be instructed to use an antibiotic-and-steroid cream or ointment for treatment — applied to the eye at least four times a day. Recovery is usually rapid (a few days). Prevention, obviously, is adequate fly control.

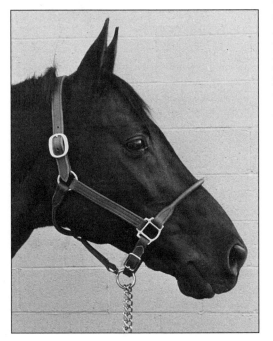

The eye normally should be clear, dark in color, with no "goop" on the eyelids or in the corner of the eye.

Other local irritations

Horses with eye irritations tend to rub their faces on stall walls or water buckets and risk further injury. Dust, dirt, plant materials and chemicals (such as fly sprays or shampoos) can cause eye irritation and sometimes allergic reactions. The symptoms of these problems are virtually identical to those for fly irritation, but it is important to get a veterinary examination to rule out other problems. Initial treatment is the same as for fly irritations.

RULE NO. 1 IN THE TREATMENT OF CORNEAL ULCERS IS NEVER TO USE OPHTHALMIC MEDICATIONS THAT CONTAIN A STEROID.

Habronemiasis

Habronemiasis is an invasion of the tissues of the eye with the larval stages of the flies of *Habronema* species (or other species). This can occur when flies feeding around the eyes have infective larval stages in their mouth parts. In addition to the usual symptoms, there may be development of tiny, hard, raised nodules in the conjunctiva of the lids, corner of the eye and the thin layer of conjunctiva that covers the sclera ("white") of the eye. In general, any case of irritative conjunctivitis that does not clear up with antibiotic-and-steroid ointment should be considered a likely case of Habronemiasis.

Treatment involves the same topical drops therapy (on the eye surface) listed above for fly and other irritations, as well as measures to kill the larvae in the tissue. Drops available through the veterinarian will kill these larvae. However, the easiest (and equally effective) approach is to use the deworming drug ivermectin — paste worm the horse exactly as you would to treat intestinal parasites. This drug is effective at eliminating immature forms of all parasites.

It also has the advantage of not subjecting the horse to additional topical treatments.

Trauma

Trauma to the eyes can occur from a direct blow or (most commonly) dirt/rocks thrown up from the hooves of other horses. The impact causes swelling of the eye and surrounding tissues, possibly even swelling of the cornea (which makes it white). The most serious is trauma that results in scratches or deeper lacerations to the cornea.

Swelling of the lids, conjunctiva and cornea caused by trauma is treated in the same way as local irritations, although flunixin meglumine or phenylbutazone is usually recommended as part of the therapy (rather than optional).

When breaks in the cornea have occurred, it is imperative these be diagnosed as rapidly as possible and intensive therapy started to prevent complications, such as infection (highly likely in horses' eyes), deep inflammation/infection and the development of worsening ulcers (a common complication of infections that get out of control and/or inadequate treatment). With corneal ulcers, the horse will be very photosensitive (he will avoid light or opening the eye).

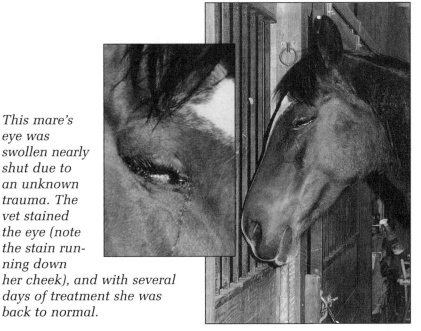

This mare's eye was swollen nearly shut due to an unknown trauma. The vet stained the eye (note the stain running down her cheek), and with several days of treatment she was back to normal.

Resistance to treatment is even more pronounced than with problems that involve only the lids/conjunctiva. An obvious whitening of the cornea will appear rapidly. Over the period of a day or so, some growth of blood vessels into the cornea will also be seen (these disappear with proper treatment). If the injury is deep, blood or white material will also appear inside the eye itself.

Rule No. 1 in the treatment of corneal ulcers is never to use ophthalmic medications that contain a steroid. These will usually be clearly labeled as having a steroid, but if you have any doubt, check with your veterinarian first. (Ophthalmic steroid medications usually contain either prednisolone or dexamethasone.)

SMALL INJURIES MAY BE VISIBLE ONLY AFTER THE EYE IS STAINED WITH FLUROSCEIN, A SPECIAL DYE.

When injuries involve the deeper layers of the cornea, an enzyme is activated that can result in the original damage becoming both wider and deeper. Injuries that go all the way through the cornea are usually associated with some loss of fluid and an eye that is at least partially collapsed/shrunken. If the hole closes over, the fluid will form again.

The biggest danger with full-thickness injuries is the formation of scar tissue within the eye that prevents the pupil from functioning normally. Scar tissue may block normal avenues of fluid flow within the eye, cause elevated pressures in the eye and increase the risk that surface infection will spread to the deep structures of the eye.

These possible complications are real possibilities, even likelihoods, if treatment is delayed or is inadequate. Permanently impaired vision, loss of vision and even loss of the eye are all possible in cases of corneal damage.

Corneal ulcers

Treatment of corneal ulcers involves intensive use of antibiotics and keeping the pupil dilated to help minimize the chances of internal scars/adhesions. Antibiotic drops or ointment will need to be applied every two to four hours around the clock until the damage shows signs of healing (i.e., reduction in size). **Failure to keep to this schedule can result in a serious infection and permanent damage.**

Atropine drops are applied every two to four hours until the pupil is well dilated, then frequency is decreased to every four to six hours. The horse must be kept in a dark stall. **Cover the windows if needed, as light is painful to the eye.** General care also includes regular, gentle removal of any mucus or other exudate that may accumulate around the eye or on the lids. Again, phenylbutazone or flunix-

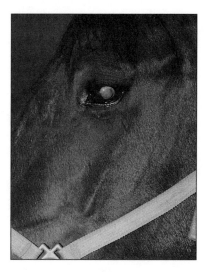

The white in this horse's eye is a corneal ulcer.

in meglumine may be used, especially in initial stages, both to keep the horse more comfortable and to help control/decrease the inflammatory response.

Even proper treatment does not guarantee healing that will proceed smoothly. Bacteria can develop resistance to the drug you are using, or infection with new strains can occur. Fungal infections are also sometimes a problem in cases of corneal damage, especially if the antibiotic treatment is effectively limiting bacterial numbers. (Bacteria normally compete with fungi.)

Your veterinarian may visit daily for the first few days, then every few days until healing is progressing nicely. Even with regular visits, you will have the important job of paying close attention to the condition of the eye, noting any changes and calling immediately with signs of possible worsening.

These signs include:
- **more swelling of the eye, greater sensitivity to light, more whitening of the cornea.**
- **increase in number of blood vessels.**
- **increase in size of the ulcer.**
- **change in color of the ulcer or the cornea.**

To accurately monitor the eye, it is important that you get a good look at it at least once a day, using a tranquilizer if necessary (call the vet for suggestions if you are having problems).

Examine the eye before you administer any medications. Write down what you see so that trends can be more easily followed, even making sketches and using some form of rough measurement (i.e., ulcer extends about 1/4 of the length of the lower lid, etc.).

Flushing eyes

It may seem like a good idea to flush the horse's eyes to remove mucus or if you suspect there is irritating material in the eye. In fact, flushing would be ideal under those circumstances and would probably provide the horse with some relief. The problem is getting the job done safely. A horse with a painful eye will resist treatment. Simply getting a few drops of medication where you want them is often a big enough challenge. Attempting to run moderately large volumes of fluid over the eye is another story entirely. The greatest danger is further injury to the eye if the horse resists (and he will) and containers, syringes, hoses, etc. are bumped against the eye.

If you feel that your horse's temperament and your specific situation (adequate facilities and personnel for restraint) would permit flushing, try the following method.

Restrain the horse so that he has an absolute minimum of freedom to move around and with the head well restrained. Find a device that will allow drainage, such as a small vegetable strainer, plastic container with holes poked in, etc. This will be your eye cup.

The eye cup must be large enough to fit over the eye with at least a half-inch margin away from the tissues of the eye in all directions. You will use one hand to hold the "eye cup" firmly in place, allowing no movement. Remember, the greatest danger with this procedure is the risk your equipment will bump into and injure the eye.

Using your other hand, gently but steadily pour at least three or four ounces of fluid into the cup over the eye creating, in effect a bath for the eye. Ideally, this should be a sterile saline solution or store-purchased eye-washing solution. Cool, clean water is the second choice. A flush of this type will cool the eye, remove adherent mucus or other material and may remove some other debris.

For most effectiveness, the eye should be treated with the lids held open and everted (turned inside out). However, this is a job you should leave to the veterinarian who can make use of such additional measures as a tranquilizer and/or anesthesia to make the procedure more safe and comfortable.

Blocked tear ducts

Eyes constantly produce tears to lubricate and wash away foreign material. Tears normally exit the eye through a tiny opening in the inner corner. They then enter a long, slender duct that runs under the mucus membrane of the nasal passages and exits at the lower end of the nose. You can easily see the nasal opening of the tear duct by looking inside the nose at the junction between the pigmented, dark tissue and the pink mucus membrane lining the nasal cavity.

A tear duct can become partially or completely blocked, causing tears to back up in the eyes and spill over onto the face. A horse may be born with this problem, but more likely it results from inflammation caused by irritation to the eye, viral or bacterial infection, allergic reactions or trauma.

To treat this problem, the veterinarian passes a fine tube up the tear duct from the nasal end. This is a fairly delicate procedure but not extremely difficult to perform as the sensation in the area is easily blocked with topical anesthetic sprays, drops or ointments. The tear duct is then flushed with sterile saline solution to attempt to

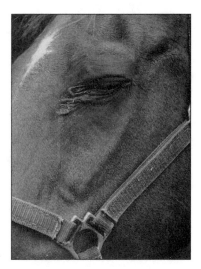

When a horse's tear duct is blocked, tears run outside the eye area and often get crusty in the corner of the eye, as dirt collects. This can be a prime feeding ground for flies.

dislodge any collection of inflammatory material (pus) that may be trapped inside. The tear duct may then be filled with an antibiotic/steroid solution, injected through the tube. You may be instructed to apply the same solution to the eye several times a day after this.

A blocked tear duct may be a one-time problem that responds to treatment, or the horse can experience repeated episodes and require periodic treatment. Although a blocked tear duct may not be a particularly serious problem in most cases, it should be treated nonetheless, as an overflow of tears will irritate the skin, causing hair loss, and because material trapped within the tear duct becomes a natural breeding ground for bacteria.

Administering eye medications

Treating eye problems requires placing either drops or ointments into the affected eye a minimum of four times per day, sometimes as often as every two to three hours around the clock. If you have ever tried to treat an eye problem in a child, you have a preview of what can be expected from your horse! The combination of the pain in the eye and the horse not being able to see what you are doing results in considerable resistance.

Since horses resent having their eye areas touched even when no problem exists, it is a good idea to practice the technique of giving eye medications before actually having to treat a horse with a sore eye. This is where having taught your horse to drop his head comes in handy.

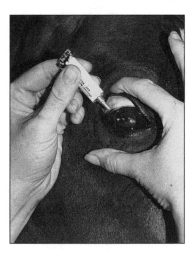

Giving eye medications is usually a two-person job — one to administer and one to restrain. The handler stands on the side opposite the eye to be treated. It sometimes helps for the handler to place a hand over the "good" eye. Grabbing a

sizable handful of skin along the neck is also fairly effective in restraining the horse, if necessary.

The person treating the eye should place one hand on the nose or halter and hold the medication bottle or tube in the other hand. The nose hand is then worked slowly up the face to eye level. Using the thumb and index finger, spread apart the upper and lower eyelids just enough to be able to see the eye itself. This step is where you will meet the most resistance.

The hand holding the medication rests just above the eye, on the bone of the orbit (socket) but not pressing on the eye or lids. This is important to prevent accidentally poking the horse in the eye with the medication tube. Aim for the opening between lower and upper lids and deposit the medication in this area by dropping it onto the surface of the eye and inner layer of the lids, but don't allow the medication bottle or tube tip to touch the eye. When finished, close the bottle or tube promptly to prevent contamination. Praise the horse generously.

Treatment of eyes tends to become more difficult over time, rather than easier. The horse learns what is going to happen and what is expected of him but doesn't become more cooperative — at least not until the pain level in the eye has decreased considerably.

For horses who become virtually impossible to safely treat in the above manner, there are three options:

- *Move the horse to a full-service hospital or clinic where treatments will be done for you. This also has the advantage of allowing any changes in the eye that require adjustments in medication to be detected quickly.*

- *The veterinarian can treat the eye on a once-a-day basis by injecting antibiotics or other medications into the filmy layer of tissue covering the sclera (the white of the eye). This is a delicate procedure, done with a tiny needle, and produces a noticeable bump or "bleb" over the surface of the sclera but under its thin outer covering. The medication will be slowly absorbed.*

■ *The veterinarian may place a segment of plastic tubing that runs from the inner surface of the eyelid, behind the ear and down the horse's neck. Medication is injected into the end of the tube on the horse's neck and runs through the tube and into the horse's eye. The tubing is heated at the eyelid end and formed into a mushroom shaped flare so that it will not pull out. Tubing has "wings" of tape sutured to the skin for further stability.*

Glossary

Cataract: *A whitening (opacity) of the normally clear lens.*

Conjunctiva: *The moist, pink inner lining of the eyelids.*

Cornea: *The outer, clear covering on the surface of the eye.*

Iris: *The colored inner portion of the eye.*

Lens: *A normally clear structure, located behind the pupil, that focuses light on the retina.*

Ophthalmic: *Pertaining to the eye.*

Optic: *Pertaining to vision.*

Panophthalmitis: *Inflammation of the entire eye.*

Pupil: *The round, black "hole" in the eye that dilates or constricts in response to light.*

Retina: *The back of the eye; the area where light and objects are perceived; location of the optic nerve.*

Sclera: *The "white" of the eye.*

Uveitis: *Inflammation of the deeper (inside) structures in the front portion of the eye.* PH

10

Why He May Be Going Blind

Fortunately, blindness in horses is relatively rare. Nevertheless, most horsepeople will be acquainted with at least one blind horse during their career.

Many of the age- or disease-related causes of blindness that afflict people and pets do not occur in horses. **Horses adapt so well to loss of vision that their owners often do not know for some time that the horse may be going blind.** In fact, some behavior problems, such as shying or refusing jumps, are caused by vision problems. The good news is that blindness does not have to end a horse's career or usefulness. We'll walk you through the common causes of blindness, treatment of eye problems and how to train a blind or going-blind horse.

Direct injury

Trauma to the horse's head may result in a loss of vision or the need for removal of the eye. Severe penetrating injuries essentially destroy the eye or make the chances of restoring it to useful function impossible. In addition, more superficial trauma to the outer eye — corneal damage — may progress rapidly to inflammation involving deeper structures, thinning and rupture of the cornea or severe infection with irreversible scarring if treatment is inadequate, improper or delayed.

Head trauma occurring at some distance from the eye can also cause vision problems related to the ripping, hemorrhage or swelling of the optic nerve — the nerve responsible for vision.

What may seem like a minor eye irritation can become a major infection, resulting in a corneal scar.

Most, if not all, cases of severe penetrating injury to the eye will not be treatable. It is important to remove the eye as soon as this is determined, to prevent unnecessary pain and infection.

Corneal injuries, even those that do not appear extensive at first, must be aggressively treated from the beginning. Symptoms include photophobia (avoidance of light), excessive tearing, keeping the eye closed and reluctance to have you approach or touch that side of the head.

The veterinarian will examine the eye directly and probably apply a special staining paper impregnated with the dye fluoroscein, which turns a bright orange color in the tears and along the edges of any damaged area of cornea.

Treatment consists of placing antibiotic drops or ointments into the eye every two to four hours for the first few days. Atropine drops or ointment may also be prescribed to help with the pain and allow the antibiotic to penetrate more deeply. The eyes should be examined by the vet every few days to determine if the antibiotic is working and that there are no signs of fungal infection, which would require special medication.

In any serious head trauma, even if it does not directly involve the eye, the eye should be carefully examined with an

ophthalmoscope for evidence of damage to the optic nerve or retina. Damage may be caused by traction on the optic nerve resulting in nerve damage and/or swelling, as well as by involvement of the retina in inflammation or damage to the retina caused by interrupted blood supply.

Regardless of the cause, treatment consists of aggressive use of corticosteroid drops or ointments, and probably systemic anti-inflammatory drugs as well (steroids, phenylbutazone, flunixine meglumine or Banamine, aspirin, etc.) in hopes of controlling and eliminating the inflammation and preventing irreversible damage.

FYI: The most common causes of blindness in horses include:

- *Recurrent uveitis ("moonblindness").*
- *Trauma.*
- *Congenital cataracts.*
- *Damage to the retina (back of the eye) and/or optic nerve caused by systemic illnesses, such as flu or strangles.*
- *Loss of blood supply to the retina caused by clots inside the feeding blood vessels.*

Cataracts

Cataracts, the opacities (whitenings) that develop inside the normally clear lens of the eye, are painless but cause blindness by preventing light from reaching the retina. **Horses do not have problems with age-related cataracts seen in humans and dogs, nor with disease-related lens problems, such as caused by diabetes or high cholesterol.** However, they do have problems with congenital (present at birth) cataracts, which may have a hereditary basis. **Veterinary ophthalmologists believe all foals should be checked for congenital cataracts before the age of one month.**

Treatment involves removal of the involved lens or lenses. Results are best when surgery is performed after the foal has been halter broken and is easier to work with (for ease of medicating the eye after surgery) but before the age of six months. Many foals go on to have serviceable vision for the rest of their lives, but the risk of complications is fairly high and the list of possible complications is long.

Retinal damage

Although uncommon, horses have developed damage to the retina following severe infections, such as influenza or a body-wide strangles infection. It is not clear if the organisms themselves cause the damage or if damage results from clotting abnormalities or injuries to blood vessels. In any case, the damage is more likely to show up as partial blindness/difficulty with sight that is not diagnosed until some time after the original infection has cleared. Because of the delay between the time when the problem begins and time of diagnosis, treatment is not likely to help.

Training the blind or going blind horse

As many know, John's horse, Bright Zip, is completely blind — the result of an anaphylactic reaction to an antibiotic injection. He's doing just fine, and John is working him on a regular basis, as he always has done.

From personal experience, John offers recommendations for working with horses who are blind or losing their sight:

Since a horse does not know where he is stepping, activities such as crossing a creek or going up and down hills must be undertaken carefully, usually one step at a time, allowing the horse to find his footing.

When I first led Zip, it was hard for me to remember that he was blind. I've been guilty of almost walking him into walls, or assuming that he sees what I'm tying him up to, and he's bumped right into it. Handling a blind horse takes a conscious adjustment on the part of the owner.

So, just as a seeing-eye dog stops before a blind person goes up or down a step, we have to indicate to our horse that he's about to go up or down inclines or even slight changes in the ground. Give him a cue — maybe pick up on the rein or lead rope — to let him know something is different in front of him. Then allow him time to feel his way.

If a horse is blind or going blind in one eye, it's extremely important that you overload the training on the good side. The cues need to be taught about three or four times better on the good side than on the blind side, because the horse is going to fade toward his blind side.

If the horse can see a 10-foot drop-off on his left, he's going to go to the right. It doesn't make any difference that there may be a 20-foot drop-off on the right. He only knows what he sees, and if he can't see anything on the right, he assumes it's OK over there. It's important that our physical cues be taught extremely well on both sides, but the good side should be trained well beyond what you would ordinarily do.

Work off physical touch and physical cues, not voice commands. Why not verbal cues? You may get into a situation in which he can't hear them or, like Zip, his hearing may be diminished as well. A verbal cue, for any horse, is a "hope and a wish" cue, not a definite command. A physical cue is much stronger than a verbal cue. With a blind horse, you can't wager safety on a verbal cue.

Blind horses are pretty easy to train. They are less spooky, because they don't see shadows and react to them.

You have to look out for your blind horse and be sure not to put him in situations where he can't fend for himself, such as turnout with other horses. If the horse knows his roommate well, or the roommate looks out for him, that may be fine. But should another horse decide to kick or bite him, he won't know it's coming. I'm careful when turning Zip out. Because we travel and he's in a different stall nearly every night and, like many blind horses, he tends to walk in circles, I tie him in the stall at night. That way I know he'll be safe, and his water and feed will be where he expects them to be.

The amazing thing about blind horses is that there are few maneuvers, other than jumping, that you can't do, as confidence builds in the rider and the horse. I work green horses off Zip, rope off him, trail ride and ride bridleless in demonstrations. It amazes me that he can gallop full out, stop and spin without losing his balance. People watching our demonstrations have a hard time believing that Zip is blind. Part of the credit goes to the fact that Zip was well-trained before he went blind, so we already had physical cues to work from.

Recurrent uveitis

ERU (equine recurrent uveitis) is a major cause of severely decreased eyesight and eventual blindness in horses. It is a complicated problem that is not completely understood.

ERU, or "moonblindness," is believed to be an autoimmune disease, meaning that the body attacks its own tissues. **Autoimmune diseases can occur when any body substance that does not normally have direct contact with the blood "spills" and is exposed to the blood cells of the immune system.** These normally isolated substances are sometimes termed "protected substances." Joint fluid and cerebrospinal fluid (the fluid bathing the brain and spinal cord) are two examples of protected substances. The contents of the eye are also protected substances — the fluids inside the eye, the lens proteins and probably other proteins.

It is believed ERU develops after an insult or infection has caused a break in the physical barriers between the contents of the eye and the blood. Antibodies to intraocular proteins then form, and the immune system begins to attack the eye just as it would attack an invading virus.

Another possibility is that antibodies are formed during an infection, which are then directed both against the invading organism and the tissue it happens to be attacking, creating a combination antibody that will react to one, either or both. **Once the process begins, the antibodies are present for the horse's life, and the horse is at high risk of repeat problems.**

A variety of known or suspected problems are believed to be capable of initiating ERU. These include:

■ Infection with the organism *Leptospira*.

■ Viral infections.

■ The parasite *Onchocerca*, which travels in the superficial layers of the skin and also causes severe dermatitis on the undersurface of the belly in warm months.

■ Bacterial or coccidial infections.

■ Possibly vaccination reactions.

■ Possibly allergies.

In many horses, the actual cause is never known.

A survey of ERU owners performed by the ERU Network showed the suspected primary cause in most horses was Leptospirosis, followed closely by "don't know," then trauma and *Onchocerca* infestation.

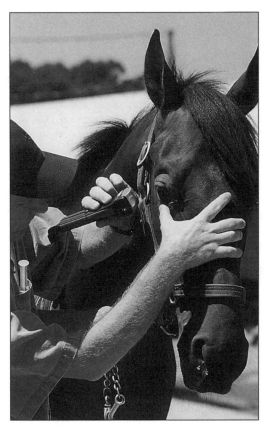

In addition, there seems to be a breed predilection for Quarter Horses and Appaloosas, although other breeds may be affected. Unfortunately, the research has not been done to determine exactly why.

Diagnosing the specifics of a problem requires close examination of the eye by a veterinarian, often along with various staining procedures.

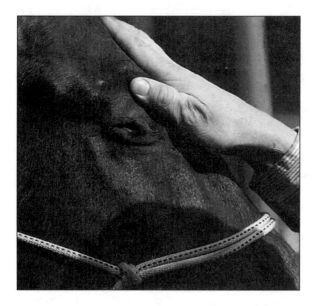

This horse lost half his eyelid in an accident. Without the natural protection of eyelid and eyelashes, he's more prone to eye irritation from dust and sun, and more reactive to things approaching his head from the right than the left.

There is no association between color, sex or age and the likelihood of having ERU. Horses develop their first signs anywhere from one year of age to over 20. Because it probably takes several months to develop after the initiating cause/infection, foals and weanlings are seldom diagnosed.

Principal early symptoms for ERU, either first episode or recurrences, are essentially the same as those for any type of eye injury/pain. Aversion to light (photophobia), keeping the eye shut and tearing are the most common, followed closely by swelling of the eye and eye lids, rubbing the eye and development of an exudate at the corners of the eyes. With ERU, examination of the eye will usually show white or blue patches on the cornea, enlarged blood vessels along the eye and in the conjunctiva, possibly blood in the interior of the eye, tightly constricted pupil and commonly the development of ulcers or breaks in the cornea.

In a nutshell, the interior of the eye becomes inflamed as a result of the immune reaction. This causes tissues to swell, blood vessels to grow into areas where they are not normally found, tissues to break down and adhesions to form between the various structures of the eye, making them lose their ability to react normally (i.e., pupils can't respond to light) and putting pressure on them, eventually tearing/damaging other structures. Other complications, such as calcium deposition in areas of damaged cornea, may also result.

After the initial attack is treated and quiets down, the horse may be symptom-free for a while, but that varies and is not predictable.

Most experts believe that during these quiet periods the eye is still abnormal, being constantly "under attack," but at a level where the anti-inflammatory mechanisms counterbalance the inflammation. Sooner or later, something upsets this delicate balance, and another "attack" of moonblindness results.

The cyclical, recurrent nature of this problem is how the term "moonblindness" originated. Early observers of the problem thought it might be related to the phases of the moon.

We do not know precisely what triggers recurrent attacks, but it seems clear that anything that stresses the horse — and therefore stresses his immune system — can trigger an attack. Among the reported triggers in the Network survey were windy conditions (surprisingly common), deworming or vaccination, shipping/trailering, dust and the stress of new stable/pasture mates. **By far, the most commonly mentioned suspected trigger was change in season.**

Spring and summer appear to be peak danger times for many horses, suggesting a link to either intensity of sunlight (more likely in light-skinned horses), emergence of flies or activation of/exposure to organisms (*Leptospira*) or parasites (*Onchocerca*) more active at these times of the year.

For most horses, ERU is a progressively downhill disease, leading to further damage to the eyes and blindness. However, aggressive treatment and management techniques can result in more rapid control of episodes, with decreased likelihood of worsening damage, or they can at least minimize the damage.

Treatment of the initial episode and acute flare-ups involves antibiotics to attack possible infectious organisms (primarily aimed at Leptospirosis), anti-inflammatories (corticosteroids and nonsteroidal anti-inflammatory drugs, such as Banamine, phenylbutazone, aspirin or others in this group), antibiotic and, possibly, steroid ointments (if the cornea is intact — no ulcers) to the eye itself.

Another possible route for drugs is subconjunctival injection — the placement of a tiny needle under the thin tissue covering the white of the eye and injection of minute amounts of medication in this location.

Other treatments, usually saved for a time when the eye has quieted down, include ivermectin to kill *Onchocerca* larvae remaining in the body and vaccination for Leptospirosis. **The ivermectin treatment is risky, since there is always a chance that larvae might be located in or near the eye, and killing them could trigger a massive immune response.** If this therapy is used, the horse should be pretreated with large doses of corticosteroids and/or other anti-inflammatories to minimize this reaction.

Leptospira vaccination is also somewhat risky. There is no approved vaccine for horses, so vets must use a bovine (cow) vaccine. Vaccination itself may trigger an ERU attack or any number of other reactions, from fever to founder. The decision to try either of these therapies is a complicated one that is best made in consultation with a veterinary ophthalmologist.

Management considerations include strict dust control, use of fly masks, avoidance of direct sun exposure in the spring and summer, avoidance of exposure to natural water sources and/or cattle (may be infected with *Leptospira*), and avoidance of stress. Many horses are also placed on long-term maintenance therapy with anti-inflammatory, such as MSM, low-dose or alternate-day corticosteroids, phenylbutazone, aspirin or Banamine.

While there is no known cure or total preventative, paying attention to the health of the eye tissues, the immune system and the horse in general will go a long way toward minimizing the severity of the problem. There is also the concern that long-term therapy with anti-inflammatories or antibiotics has the potential for very real negative health consequences.

Holistic therapy

Rapidly growing in acceptance is the application of non-drug treatments for horses with ERU. Consider these reasonable approaches:

Vitamin C — *4.5 to 7.0 grams daily — boosts immune system, strengthens capillaries.*

Bioflavinoids — *(hesperidin complex) 20,000+ mg/day — complements vitamin C, strengthens capillaries.*

Grape-seed extract — *minimum 600 mg/day — potential anti-inflammatory, antioxidant; strengthens capillaries.*

Vitamin A — *natural sources (carrots, alfalfa) — the most important vitamin for vision.*

Vitamin E — *2000 IU/day — important antioxidant.*

Trace Mineral — *supplement to include copper, zinc, manganese, selenium; important to the functioning of the body's own anti-inflammatory/antioxidant enzyme systems.*

*Other herbal or homeopathic treatments or remedies may
also be tried, including such things as bilberry and N-
acetylcysteine. We do not suggest you consider these as a
substitute for pharmaceutical medications. Flare-ups are
serious and require aggressive treatment. You may, however, look into the alternatives for maintenance and support during acute episodes by locating a certified holistic
veterinary practitioner through one of the following sources:*

Academy of Veterinary Homeopathy (AVH)
305-652-1590
www.acadvethom.org

American Holistic Veterinary Medical Assoc. (AHVMA)
410-569-0795
www.altvetmed.com

Support groups

Support for owners of horses with moonblindness
Owners of horses with ERU can find useful management tips, the
latest in background information on causes, updates on therapy
and a list of veterinarians who have experience treating this disease by contacting the ERU Network. The Network, headed by
Mary G. Nelson, is intended to educate horse people about recurrent uveitis and provide a forum for owners and treating veterinarians. Those interested should write to Mary at 18 Lake Drive,
Mendham, NJ 07945. ▣

Notes

11

Diarrhea Dangers

We tend to consider diarrhea more of a nuisance than a significant health problem. However, diarrhea in horses can be serious, even life-threatening, and may have long-term complications.

iarrhea can have many causes. The way it is treated and how serious a problem it is initially or in the long run depend on several factors, including the horse's age, general condition when the problem started and the cause of the diarrhea. **Diarrhea in foals and older horses is potentially more serious than in healthy young adults.** However, severe diarrhea is always a serious problem.

When is diarrhea serious?

Diarrhea of a watery consistency that sprays out of the horse under pressure should be considered an emergency if it is present for more than one bowel evacuation. Diarrhea of this nature commonly can be ejected in a jet-like stream that extends for several feet, hitting nearby walls at the level of the horse's anal opening and causing unmistakable diarrhea stains on the stall wall.

This is a serious diarrhea because the horse's intestinal tract contains huge amounts of fluid — some of which the horse took in and some of which was secreted by the digestive system. Under normal circumstances, this fluid passes along the intestines in a gradual, orderly fashion. The large intestine (colon and cecum) extracts vital electrolytes and other nutrients, as well as a significant amount of water, gradually drying the manure as it passes

Diarrhea in young foals can be life-threatening. Action should be taken quickly to prevent dehydration if you suspect a diarrhea problem.

along the intestine, until the end result is the familiar well-formed soft ball of fecal material.

When diarrhea is watery, dehydration and electrolyte imbalances result rapidly. Even if the horse is drinking normal or greater-than-normal amounts of water, he will not be able to keep up with the losses. Also, diarrhea of this nature is more likely to be caused by a viral or bacterial infection, which can make the horse very ill and could be spread to other horses, even to humans.

Diarrhea that is not watery, but is softer than normal and not formed into balls, poses less of an immediate threat to the horse in terms of dehydration and electrolyte losses. **The horse who is otherwise well, eating and drinking normally, can remain essentially stable as long as he is not stressed in any way.** However, a horse with this type of diarrhea has little fluid or electrolyte reserve and always hovers on the brink of dehydration or mineral imbalance. Furthermore, this type of diarrhea signals a serious imbalance in the intestinal tract, which will eventually rob the horse of the ability to efficiently digest and absorb the feed he takes in, especially hays. **If a horse develops abnormally soft manure that persists for greater than two days, steps should be taken to determine both the cause and cure.**

In determining how much of an emergency diarrhea may be, look at other symptoms the horse may have. Indicators of a serious problem that requires immediate attention include:

■ Fever.

■ Depression or anxiety.

■ Changes in the color of the mucus membranes of the lips: A red, blue or gray discoloration indicates toxins or bacteria in the horse's bloodstream. A yellow color (jaundice) appears in horses that have been significantly off their feed for 24 hours or more.

■ Evidence of dehydration. Check the inside of the horse's mouth. It should feel moist. If dry and sticky, the horse is dehydrated.

You can also use the "pinch test" to check for dehydration. Pick up a fold of skin along the horse's neck, then release it. If hydration (amount of water in the body) is normal, the fold will be difficult to pick up and the skin will quickly return to a normal position. **If it remains up in a tent for a few seconds, the horse is dehydrated.**

NOTE: This test should be used to back up the findings on examination of the mouth, a more sensitive test. In older horses especially, skin elasticity or "springiness" is not what it is in a young animal, and tenting of the skin can occur to some degree without dehydration.

■ Hooves that feel colder or hotter than normal, with or without any signs of lameness: Laminitis (founder) is a common complication of any intestinal problem. Hooves that feel very cold can be in the early stages of laminitis, when blood flow to the feet is shut down by constriction (closing down) of the blood vessels. Cold feet can also indicate shock. Hot hooves and lameness occur at a later stage of founder.

■ Abdominal pain/colic: **Any horse showing abdominal pain symptoms/behavior changes should be examined by your veterinarian.** These include sweating, turning around to look at the belly, tail elevated — with or without passage of gas — kicking at the belly, pawing, laying down (will often lie quietly with only mild pain), standing stretched out as if attempting to urinate, and rolling, which may indicate moderate to severe pain.

■ Decreased water/food consumption: **Horses with intestinal disorders commonly go off their grain.** This is an instinctive attempt to reduce the load of energy-rich feeds that become toxic if not properly digested. As long as the horse is eating hay well, this is not a problem, although treatment should be initiated for the diarrhea to get the horse back on his normal feed. Decreased water consumption, or normal water intake along with signs of increasing dehydration, is a problem since the horse could dehydrate rapidly.

Causes of diarrhea

Parasites: Diarrhea caused by intestinal parasites ("worms") tends to be more common in young animals and older, especially debilitated horses, but it can occur at any age. Fecal examinations to detect eggs may be deceptively negative, since it is often the immature forms, which do not lay eggs, that cause the problem.

Parasites can cause diarrhea by directly damaging the lining of the intestines, which is then unable to properly absorb nutrients, water and electrolytes, or by causing abnormal motility in the intestinal tract, which results in deeper damage to the intestinal wall.

THE MOST COMMON CAUSE OF CHRONIC DIARRHEA IS AN IMBALANCE IN THE ORGANISMS INHABITING THE INTESTINAL TRACT.

Viruses: Rotavirus is a well-documented and serious intestinal viral infection, usually restricted to foals. It can cause rapid dehydration, shock and death. It is more likely than other viruses (such as a flu virus) to have intestinal manifestations in addition to the more familiar respiratory-tract problems, but this is not well documented. These can infect horses of all ages.

Viral diarrheas will always have an associated phase when the horse is running a fairly high fever. **However, the fever may go unnoticed as it often occurs before the other symptoms and/or may only be present in cycles throughout the day.** Failure to nurse or eat well will also often occur in advance of the diarrhea. **Any foal or older horse who is not eating or drinking well should have its temperature taken.** Documenting that the horse had a fever before the diarrhea started will help the veterinarian in make a diagnosis.

Bacteria: The intestine normally hosts a wide variety of bacteria, the majority of which are friendly and beneficial, playing roles in the digestion of plant materials and the breakdown of undigested/undigestible portions of the diet.

However, there are also a number of potentially deadly bacteria that exist both inside the intestinal tract and in the environment. Some of these are capable of causing diarrhea and serious illness even in a healthy, well-balanced intestinal tract. Others do not become a problem unless they gain access to the intestinal tract of a foal (where normal populations of beneficial bacteria have not yet been established). An adult horse who has any intestinal upset that results in the normal populations of beneficial bacteria being reduced or killed off may also be at risk. This removes competition from the harmful bacteria and/or changes the composition of the intestinal fluid in such a way that it becomes more favorable for the harmful bacteria to grow.

Ration Plus helps create an environment conducive to the growth of healthy bacteria.

Other organisms: The diarrhea of Potomac horse fever is caused by an organism named *Erlichia*. Although researchers disagree on the point, there may also be strains of protozoa that are capable of causing diarrhea. Protozoa are larger than bacteria — they are the actively moving organisms you can see under a microscope in a drop of typical pond water. **Large numbers of beneficial protozoa normally exist in the intestinal tract of the horse and assist in digestion of coarse plant materials.**

Dietary: Rapid changes in diet, even turnout onto rich grasses, can easily cause some diarrhea.

Treatment of acute diarrhea

Fluids are an important part of the treatment of diarrhea. If the animal is still drinking well, addition of an electrolyte product to the water may also be recommended. Electrolyte formulas that are specifically made for diarrhea cases are usually the best to use, since they take into account the specific metabolic changes that diarrhea can induce.

Your veterinarian may also check blood samples to get exact levels of all the important electrolytes and then recommend a specific mixture be used. As with any oral electrolyte replacement, it is important that fresh water be offered at the same time. Horses who refuse to take in the electrolytes, or are more severely dehydrated and cannot keep up with the need by voluntary intake, may need to have fluids and electrolytes administered by stomach tube and/or intravenously until hydration has improved.

Oral antibiotics are never used in horses for diarrhea because the antibiotic will kill off beneficial bacterial populations, probably in larger numbers than any offending harmful bacteria, which would make it easier for the harmful strains to flourish and multiply. Even intravenous or intramuscular antibiotics are usually avoided unless it is the veterinarian's judgment that the bacteria have actually gained access to the bloodstream. Antibiotics given intravenously or intramuscularly (especially tetracycline) can also find their way to the intestinal tract and kill beneficial strains. In fact, sometimes diarrhea problems develop as a result of giving antibiotics for another problem.

With severe diarrhea where bacterial toxins are believed to be playing a role, efforts are usually made to bind some of these toxins with medications. The veterinarian may administer charcoal by stomach tube. Pepto-Bismol, or a generic equivalent, is also sometimes recommended. The active ingredient in Pepto-Bismol is bismuth, which binds toxins. Other non-medicated, no antibiotic agents containing several ingredients active in binding toxins are also used. Most are manufactured for foals or calves but are just as appropriate for adult horses, with adjustment of the dose. They are good to keep on hand, but you should always consult with the veterinarian before giving any diarrhea treatments, even if you think the cause is something simple like a diet change.

Salmonella

Salmonella is one of the most serious bacterial diarrheas. Salmonella organisms exist in the environment and possibly also along the normal intestinal tract but in small numbers that cannot compete with the much larger populations of beneficial bacteria in a healthy intestinal tract. In addition, there are some strains of salmonella that are so virulent (capable of causing disease) that they can override even the defenses of a healthy intestinal tract.

Salmonella infections are almost always associated with severe, body-wide problems that make the horse extremely ill. Another important feature of salmonella bacteria is that the disease can be spread rapidly to other horses as well as to other animals and humans.

The salmonella organism produces a potent poison, called an endotoxin. Under normal conditions, an endotoxin cannot gain access to the body across the protective barrier of the intestinal tract. In fact, small amounts of endotoxins can be found along the intestines of normal animals without any ill effects.

It is not clear exactly what causes the protective mechanism to break down with salmonella infections, but once it does, trouble starts. The endotoxin sets in motion a severe inflammatory reaction at the level of the intestines, which causes large amounts of fluid and electrolytes to be secreted into the intestine. This is the body's attempt to dilute the offending toxin and flush it out of the intestines. The result is diarrhea.

The endotoxin also damages the walls of blood vessels, causing them to leak vital body proteins. Without these proteins in the blood, the blood cannot attract and hold sufficient amounts of water. Blood volume drops below normal. Dehydration and shock result. Endotoxin is also spread throughout the body. The horse develops fever, dehydration, red mucus membranes, elevated pulse and respiratory rates and blood-clotting abnormalities. As a result of endotoxins damaging blood vessels to the feet, laminitis/founder is a common complication of salmonella (or any other severe bacterial infection) — almost unavoidable in severe cases.

Carriers of salmonella can appear perfectly healthy but contaminate their environment as they shed the bacteria periodically.

Salmonella infections can also result in a state of chronic diarrhea in animals that survive the initial course of the disease. This may be due to a persistent infection and/or to disturbances in the populations of normal organisms in the intestine. Foals (and probably older horses as well) can also develop gastric (stomach) ulcers and liver damage from salmonella infections.

Horses that survive an acute salmonella infection can develop what is called a carrier state. The horse may appear to be well but still harbors significant numbers of salmonella bacteria along his intestinal tract. There may or may not be intermittent problems with diarrhea on a chronic basis. Even without repeated bouts of diarrhea, carrier horses are a constant source of contamination with salmonella bacteria and pose a health threat to other animals — and people — on the premises.

Salmonella can also become well established in the ground on a farm and has caused people to sell and move their operation. Following strict isolation procedures when dealing with an acute case of watery diarrhea can go a long way in preventing the spread of this infection between horses and contamination of the premises.

Isolation procedures

When a horse develops an acute diarrhea, especially with any other signs of serious diarrhea, it is always a good idea to institute isolation precautions until an infectious cause can be ruled out. **Ideally, the horse should be confined to a stall and have no direct contact with other horses, in a separate building or even paddock with shelter.** If this is not possible, all horses will have to be presumed to be at least exposed, if not infected, and measures taken to prevent any further possible spread. These measures include:

■ Hoof baths containing appropriate disinfectants to clean boots/shoes immediately upon leaving the stall (or other area) where the horse(s) is confined.

■ No interchange of grooming or feeding equipment or direct body contact between affected horses and other horses.

■ No access to infected animals or premises by cats or dogs.

■ Strict hand washing and changing of clothing after working around affected animals. (A set of coveralls over your other clothing can be used, then removed and hung in a secure location between uses, then washed at the end of the day.)

■ Clean the stall of affected animals last. Cover or burn possibly contaminated bedding. Wash pitchforks, wheelbarrows, etc. after use with hot, soapy water and an appropriate disinfectant. A quick call to your local farm supply store will almost certainly turn up an appropriate disinfectant product.

With some highly infectious bacterial strains, you may have to dig up the top 10 to 12 inches of dirt where the affected animal was kept and replace it to completely eliminate the organism. All walls, buckets, etc. inside the stall must be disinfected as well.

Treatment of chronic diarrhea

Chronic diarrhea, whether bouts of occasional watery diarrhea or a near-constant softening of the manure to more of a cow-manure consistency, can be difficult to treat. **Horses with this problem are always in a precarious water-and-electrolyte balance and may not tolerate stress of any kind without going "over the edge" into dehydration and electrolyte imbalances.**

The first step is to try to determine the cause. A chronic salmonella infection should be ruled out by taking several stool cultures. However, salmonella can be notoriously difficult to culture, so be prepared to do a minimum of three cultures. Chronic diarrhea may also be caused by an inability of the intestine to properly digest certain foods (malabsorption syndrome) or by invasion of the wall of the intestine by cancer (usually lymphosarcoma). In both of these cases, weight loss/loss of condition is a prominent feature.

The most common cause of chronic diarrhea is an imbalance in the organisms inhabiting the intestinal tract. We do not really know how these cases get started — maybe a heavy parasite burden, maybe an acute bacterial infection

Re-Sorb's blend of electrolytes is suited to diarrhea problems.

or even a chronic infection of some type. In any event, the horse is left with a chronic soft-manure problem, which can become worse if he is stressed. Weight loss and dehydration may occur, but some horses maintain their condition well despite this.

Microscopic examination of the fluid extracted from the manure may disclose changes in the types of bacteria present and increased or decreased numbers of protozoa.

Some horses will respond and develop normal manure again after being turned out to pasture for several months. The combination of highly digestible, natural food (grass) and allowing the horse to repopulate his intestine with beneficial organisms gradually, by exposure to the environment, seems to do the trick.

Treatment may also be attempted with a prescription oral drug called Rheaform. This compound is active against certain forms of protozoa. Many chronic diarrhea cases respond to Rheaform but will relapse again if the drug is not given continuously.

Another approach with some success is transfaunation. Normal intestinal fluid, rich in micro-organisms, is collected from horses that have been euthanized and given to the patient by stomach tube.

Use of probiotic products may also help with chronic diarrhea cases. However, many of these contain limited numbers of bacterial species, some only one. We have found a better approach is to use Ration Plus, since it encourages the growth of the beneficial bacteria, allowing the normal variety to repopulate the intestines. ▣

12

Fight & Win Against EPM

*Despite the many mysteries surrounding EPM,
certain strategies can help
minimize your horses' risk of infection.*

"**EPM is the most common equine neurologic disease in North America,**" says David Granstrom, DVM, Ph.D., an assistant director at the American Veterinary Medicine Association. In fact, across much of America half of all horses may have been exposed to EPM. Granstrom is quick to note, however, that the incidence of actual disease may be fewer than one in a 100 horses. EPM (equine protozoal myeloencephalitis) is a debilitating disease of the central nervous system (brain and spinal cord).

Granstrom, who previously piloted EPM research at Gluck Equine Research Center at the University of Kentucky, explains that the EPM perpetrator, *Sarcocystis neurona*, is a microscopic parasitic protozoan that normally cycles between opossums and probably birds. Opossum feces contain the life stage of the parasite that is infective. Birds feed on the feces, and opossums feed on dead birds, and the organism becomes active again in the opossum's digestive tract.

For some reason, it doesn't bother either the opossum or the birds, but horses, for whom it is a problem, may pick it up when grazing or drinking in areas contaminated by opossum droppings. It is also believed that bagged grains and baled hays can carry infective *Sarcocystis* organisms.

Horses are known as "dead-end hosts." This means the organism cannot spread to other horses by an infected horse. Once inside the horse, the organism is either prevented from migrating around inside the horse by the immune system or it manages to find its way to the central nervous system (CNS). For reasons that are not entirely clear, the parasite prefers and thrives in the CNS. Once there, it continues to multiply by asexual reproduction. This preferential location explains the various symptoms.

What does EPM look like?

Symptoms vary widely, from gait abnormalities and muscle wasting to facial paralysis and personality changes.

EPM can sometimes be difficult to diagnose, even go unsuspected, when the horse is not showing dramatic symptoms. While gait and balance problems are the most dramatic manifestation of EPM, the symptoms depend upon where in the horse's CNS the organism is located. The CNS includes all parts of the brain, as well as the entire length of the spinal cord. Organisms located only in the back (tail-end) portion of the spinal cord will cause symptoms limited to the back legs, back, pelvis and tail. Above this level, spinal-cord infection will cause either back-leg signs only, possibly front-leg signs only or both front-and-back-leg signs.

Spinal-cord symptoms include loss of coordination (with abnormal gait), difficulty rising, difficulty backing, difficulty circling, difficulty side-stepping, abnormal reflexes and probably other problems we cannot diagnose, since the horse can't tell us what he feels or senses. This includes such things as changes in sensation and loss of "proprioception."

Proprioception is the ability to perceive where a leg is located in space without looking at it. (Like what the doctor tests if you are asked to touch your finger to the tip of your nose with your eyes closed.) These spinal cord-related symptoms are the ones most people think of when they hear EPM. This is understandable, since they are the most dramatic and the most obvious. However, they are not the entire story.

EPM infection of the brain can cause a wide range of symptoms, depending on where the lesion is located. The best guess as to how long it takes a horse to develop symptoms after ingesting the EPM organism is a minimum of about two weeks. Several factors can influence this. If the horse only picked up a small number of organisms, symptoms would probably not appear until they had either reached a critical area or their numbers had increased to the point that the damage they were doing was extensive.

For example, a tiny number of parasites that just happened to take up residence in the area of the brain that controls vision could produce a dramatic blindness (with no other signs) in a fairly short period of time.

If that same number of parasites was scattered widely throughout the whole brain and spinal cord, symptoms could begin with subtle changes, such as slight clumsiness or the horse not balancing or moving as well on one side. These signs are easily missed or dismissed as the horse not paying attention, needing more work in a certain direction, being "one-sided" or being "sour."

Cranial nerve signs

The cranial nerves are 12 paired (right and left) large nerves that originate in the brain and serve the head. They are responsible for all the major senses (hearing, sight, taste, smell) and also supply the muscles of the head. Cranial nerve signs/symptoms include any:

■ *Change in vision.*

■ *Change in sensitivity to sound.*

■ *Abnormalities in opening or closing the eyes.*

This pony's ear droops because cranial nerves have been damaged.

■ *Drooling saliva.*

■ *Difficulty swallowing feed or water (including "choke").*

■ *Drooping eyelids, abnormal pupils or abnormally reactive pupils.*

■ *Altered sensation in the face (best checked by covering the eye and using the tip of a pen or other small blunt object to gently touch the skin of that side of the face).*

> ■ *Drooping nostrils or lips, paralyzed nostrils or lips (can be one-sided), abnormal tongue movements*
>
> ■ *Drooping ear, loss of muscle mass anywhere on the face (most obvious in the cheeks, when they are involved)*
>
> ■ *Dropping of feed, wadding up of hay or grain in the mouth.*

Sources of infection

In addition to opossum feces, horses probably become infected through bird droppings, although it's still unclear which species of birds are involved (common barnyard fowl — chickens, ducks, geese and turkeys — are not hosts for this parasite). "We know that a fair number of sporocysts pass through birds, still infective," says Granstrom. "But we don't know how big a contribution that is, and if it's a true risk for infection in horses."

Studies have also shown that insects, such as roaches and flies, can be "transport" hosts, carrying protozoa from bird and 'possum feces to horses' feed, although it's unknown how significant this risk actually is.

In theory, just one sporocyst could infect a horse with EPM. Granstrom explains, "If unchecked by the body, one sporocyst will release four sporozoites. Each sporozoite could potentially penetrate the gut, enter the bloodstream, make it to the central nervous system and begin to divide, producing 40 or 50 or 100 more. Those 40 to 100 do the same thing, over and over and over. So left unchecked, in the course of a few weeks, you could have a dead horse." Scientists estimate, however, that it actually takes large numbers

Some think they are ugly, some think they are cute. Looks aside, an opossum who visits your barn may be carrying a parasite that could be deadly to your horse.

of sporocysts — as many as millions — for clinical infection to occur, depending on the strength of each horse's immune system.

Research has shown that the organism thrives best in moderate temperature and humidity areas, and it dies easily in areas of extreme heat, cold, wet or drought. Thus, you see more outbreaks in moderate areas such as Ohio and fewer in Arizona.

When any parasite, bacterium or virus attempts to gain access to the horse's body, the horse's immune system is activated. Since such a large number of horses have antibodies to EPM in their blood, most normal, healthy animals must be able to fight off the infestation. Of the small percentage that cannot, those who go on to develop symptoms of EPM, some are believed to be immunocompromised (a fancy term for having a less-than-ideal immune response). In many cases, the suspected reason is stress.

Other influences

Other factors that could decrease the horse's immune response include a current or recent infection, vaccination, drugs and young age (immature immune system), though vaccinations, age or drugs alone do not usually compromise the immune system sufficiently to the point of making the horse vulnerable to EPM.

Most significant, however, would be inadequate nutrition. Something as simple as inadequate intake of calories (a "negative energy balance"), easily identified as the horse losing weight, can decrease immune response, since the body will divert available nutrients to such critical life-sustaining functions as keeping the brain and heart going.

Inadequate total protein intake or inadequate intake of specific amino acids can also negatively impact the immune system. And, on the vitamin-and-mineral front, vitamins C, E and A play important roles in immune responses. Zinc and selenium are also important to immune function.

Vulnerability to EPM or any infection is a good example of a situation where inadequate intake of any of these nutrients may not be enough to threaten the horse's life directly or cause some deficiency-specific disease but is enough to cause vital systems (in this case, the immune system) to function at less-than-optimal levels.

It is also possible that those horses who go on to develop symptoms of EPM represent horses who were exposed to a particularly large number of parasites, sufficiently large to "sneak past" or overwhelm even a good immune response.

Testing for EPM

EPM testing relies primarily on detection of antibodies to the EPM organism. A positive blood test indicates the horse has been exposed to EPM and has made antibodies against it. This does not mean he has the disease.

A CSF test, obtained by spinal tap, is more definitive but carries too much risk to be considered routine. It's important to understand the following reports and what they mean diagnostically.

■ *Negative blood test: No exposure to EPM. No chance of EPM-related disease unless infection occurred less than two weeks before the test. If horse is showing symptoms, should retest in two to three weeks.*

■ *Positive blood test: Horse has been exposed to EPM. This test cannot predict if the horse will ever develop symptoms; it only tells you the horse has been exposed. If the horse is showing symptoms, CSF and/or pcRNA testing (detects bits of genetic material in the CSF which are specific for the organism) should be done.*

■ *Positive CSF: EPM organisms have gained access to the central nervous system. The horse has EPM; however, OR a "false positive" may indicate a contamination of the CSF sample by positive blood.*

■ *Negative CSF: EPM organisms have not gained access to the central nervous system, OR the antibodies have not developed yet.*

Diagnosis

Generally the veterinarian is called out because the horse is exhibiting some form of neurological deficiency. But, perhaps as many as 20 other diseases or conditions have clinical signs similar to EPM, so EPM should not be suspected every time a horse moves in an uncoordinated manner or exhibits signs of cranial nerve abnormalities.

If the veterinarian suspects EPM, one of two tests are done. The blood test, which is less expensive and the easiest of the two samples to obtain is also the least informative.

The other test is on CSF fluid, obtained by means of a spinal tap. This procedure requires the horse to be very steady or tranquilized. While it is usually definitive in determining EPM, it carries too much risk and cost to be considered routine, such as accompanying pre-purchase examinations.

Treatment

The mainstay of treatment for EPM is an antiprotozoal combination of pyrimethamine and a sulfonamide drug. "Sulfonamide" refers to a group of several sulfa drugs and is not the name of a specific drug. Both drugs inhibit the growth of protozoa but do not kill them entirely. For this reason, the initial course of treatment should extend for a minimum of three months.

The inability of this combination to actually kill the protozoa is why some horses have relapses even after three months of therapy and require additional or even indefinite treatment.

Side effects of treatment include suppression of the horse's bone marrow caused by a block in folic acid metabolism, which is also how the drugs interfere with the organism. This can be prevented by giving supplemental folic acid. The horse can use the supplemental folic acid but the protozoa cannot.

The latest news on treatment is that a drug named Diclazuril is currently being tested for its efficacy in treating EPM. Researchers stress that they are only at preliminary stages of testing, and toxicity has not been established.

So much for EPM treatment. What can you do to prevent EPM or to help your horse fend off the EPM parasite, should he come in contact with it?

Boost your horse's defense system

Your first priority in escaping EPM is to ensure your horse's overall health. **Sick or stressed horses are more vulnerable to infection. Be sure to keep your horses regularly dewormed and up-to-date on vaccinations.**

Recent data suggests that EPM may fluctuate by season. Although opossums don't hibernate, they're less likely to find large sources of food in winter. **Researchers have found that sporocysts die in both freezing weather and in hot, dry weather. Sunlight will also eventually kill them.**

Granstrom suspects, however, that infection may be related more to seasonal management stresses — intensive training, long-distance hauling, pregnancy, periodic competitions — than to seasonal elements.

Studies have shown that 60 percent of EPM horses are three years old or younger. "A combination of factors probably make young horses more susceptible to infection," says Granstrom. "We hope that repeated exposure helps make them more resistant, and that young animals simply haven't had time to build up immunity. There's also some fairly stressful events in a horse's early years, such as weaning and training."

Practice good stable hygiene. Keep feed troughs and water buckets clean and clear of foreign matter — particularly bird droppings or small-animal dung. Also, don't use rain run-off from the barn roof to fill your water trough. Rooftop bird droppings can contaminate the water.

Pull up the welcome mat

The best way to reduce your horse's exposure to infective protozoa is to keep trespassing critters off your property. If birds and 'possums are infesting your facilities, physically exclude them with screens and doors.

Although small-mesh fencing around your pasture may discourage nonchalant opossums, without an electric wire across the top of the fence, they will simply scramble over it. They aren't likely to dig under a fence, however.

Scent repellents, which must be reapplied frequently, are seldom effective nor practical long-term. Also, don't be tempted to try high-frequency noise devices as deterrents. "They don't work," firmly states Harold Harlan, Ph.D., staff entomologist at the National Pest Control Association in Dunn Loring, Va. "Nor do electromagnetic fields. Animals become habituated to them very quickly."

Actually, a good watch dog is your best deterrent, since coyotes and foxes are among opossums' natural predators. And barn cats are an excellent deterrent for birds who'd otherwise roost and poop in your barn. Pet food is a prime attraction for opossums, so if you feed your pets near the barn, leave food out only during the day.

While it may be impossible to blockade all your borders, you can reduce the attractions that lure 'possums onto your property.

■ Keep horse feed in tightly closed bins. Clean up grain spills and leftover meals immediately. Avoid on-the-ground feed pans, which can tip over, leaving grain scattered.

■ Keep food-related garbage in tightly covered trash containers as far away from your horses as you can.

■ Distance your manure piles from the barn. They can also entice opossums, who scratch through horse droppings looking for undigested grain and fly maggots. To reduce fly maggots, put a good fly-control system in place or add a feed-through fly-inhibitor product to your horse's ration.

Feed and water left out for barn cats and dogs may attract opossums.

■ Remove fruit trees and berry bushes from your pastures. Persimmons, peaches, plums, apples and blackberries are particularly appealing to 'possums.

■ Eliminate access to backyard bird feeders as well as barnyard fowl feeders. Eggs, chicks and ducklings are tasty 'possum treats, so be sure your fowl have "safe houses" at night.

■ To discourage opossums from sticking around, plug up all animal burrows, and clear away brush piles from pastures. During the day, opossums will sometimes hunker down in drainage culverts or brush piles, but they prefer to sleep in underground dens.

Get to know your opossums

About the size of a large house cat, the North American opossum (Didelphis virginiana) looks like an overgrown rat. Grown opossums can measure up to 40" long, almost half of which is tail. Nocturnal creatures, opossums are seldom spotted in daylight. Frequent traffic victims at night, they're most often seen dead on the roadside.

The adaptable opossum thrives in habitats up to about 10,000 feet, except deserts. "In hospitable areas," says Steve Austad, a professor of zoology at the University of

Idaho and an opossum expert, "opossums are renowned for ranging widely, as much as a square mile or so, depending on the type of habitat. Unless they find a large food source, such as a garbage dump, opossums don't settle down for long." Instead, they just meander wherever the scent of food takes them. And despite their small brains, opossums have excellent memories for places where they've found food in the past. So, if a 'possum finds delectables in your barn, you can bet he'll be back.

Opossums will eat just about anything. They prefer animal matter (insects, slugs, worms, baby birds, mice, frogs, eggs and carrion), though they also eat mushrooms, fruits and grains. Persimmons and grapes are favorites, as are pet foods and garbage scraps.

For horse owners, it's particularly important to know where opossums poop. "They poop wherever they happen to be, whenever they need to go," said Austad. "However, they do quite often poop while they're eating." Which means, if a 'possum gets into your feed bin or berry brambles, he'll likely leave a deposit before he moseys on.

You're not likely to spot opossum poop outside, however. Opossum feces disintegrate quickly. "Opossums have a reptile-like system that mixes their urine and feces together, so it all comes out in a kind of paste," Austad says.

Opossums typically live alone, although several may share a territory. Population density depends on the locale. "In typical horse country," says Austad, "you'll find no more than one opossum for every two or three acres, unless there's a female that's ready to mate, in which case eight or 10 males may be following her around. But that would be fairly temporary, since mating season is only about two weeks in February and two weeks in June."

Fortunately, opossums are among the shortest-lived mammals, for their size, in the world. "Most live between a year and a year-and-a-half," Austad states. "It's exceptional for opossums to live two years in the wild."

Not so great, however, is that opossums are prolific reproducers. Females normally bear two litters a year. While the average litter size is about seven to eight, often no more than two survive.

Take 'em alive

To remove persistent 'possums from your property, the most humane approach is live trapping. Poisons are indiscriminate killers, putting children, horses and pets at risk, while leghold traps can expose you (and your pets) to dangerous contact with injured, frightened and possibly frenzied wild animals.

Before you start live trapping, however, check with your state wildlife resources authorities and the local office of the U.S. Fish and Wildlife Service. If protected or endangered species live in your area, you may be limited to certain kinds of traps. The trapping of certain fur-bearers may also be controlled.

A cage-like mesh trap with one door and a treadle trigger (which springs the trap closed when the animal steps on the treadle) is the simplest and safest way to trap. Harlan recommends an 8" x 8" x 24" or a 9" x 9" x 30" trap. "If your trap is too small and it closes on the animal's hind end, where the animal can back out and escape, you'll end up with an opossum that's trap-shy in the future."

Harlan's all-purpose bait includes a dollop of peanut butter, a leaf or two of lettuce, a couple of sardines, freshly cut apple and corn chips.

Arrange bait ingredients in an old cup or tuna can, and then tie the can down, either behind the trap's trigger or to the trigger itself. You can also wrap your baits in a gauze "package" to suspend over the trigger. Position the bait so as to discourage animals from reaching in from the outside and robbing the trap.

Position your traps at known pathways, at barn entrances, or under fruit trees or berry brambles. Don't bother camouflaging the cage —

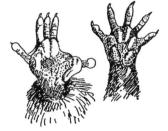

Watch for opossum tracks in the dust or mud around your barn. Their hind paws leave a distinctive print (the only kind like it in North America), with a clawless "thumb" that juts out on the inside of the print, like a distorted hand.

opossums will walk straight into a bare trap. Harlan does recommend anchoring the trap, however, either with a weight on top or by tethering it to a fence post or tree trunk. If the trap's mesh is large enough, the animal will simply stick its feet out and go, taking trap and all.

You got him...now what?

If you do decide to live-trap your 'possums, be aware that it's a long-term, on-going project. "Even if you haul them off 50 miles away," says Austad wryly, "others will move in." Also keep in mind: After you remove all opossums, it still may be a year before infective sarcocysts from old 'possum poop die off. ▣

Our thanks to contributing writer Liz Nutter.

13

Founder: Causes and Care

*You hear the diagnosis — "founder" or "laminitis" —
and even without the details,
you know it's bad!*

The foot is considered by many veterinarians to be the horse's "shock organ" — the part of the body that can be expected to show problems if an animal is severely stressed. In people, stress may appear as a headache, ulcer or heart disease, or bad nails — depending on the individual's system. **In the horse, many types of stress may take their toll on the horse's hooves.**

One reason the feet are so sensitive is the extensive network of tiny blood vessels inside the hooves. These blood vessels maintain the health and strength of the laminae, the frond-like projections of tissue that are woven into the inner surface of the hoof wall and bind it securely in place. This intricate network of blood vessels is also part of the shock-absorbing system of the hoof, expanding and contracting as the horse moves.

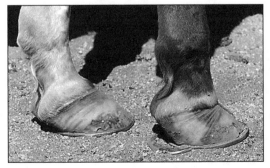

With founder, inflammation and fluid collection in the laminae cause pain and can tear them loose from their attachment to the hoof wall, causing the coffin bone to pull away toward the sole.

Anywhere you find a rich supply of vessels, you will also find a lot of nerves. Nerves always accompany blood vessels, and they assist in regulating how much blood flows into an area and how rapidly it flows out. Nerves also sense pain. We all know how painful it is when a fingertip gets caught in a door or hit by a hammer. Take this pain and imagine how much worse it would be if you were forced to use that pounding fingertip to support your weight, and you will begin to get some idea of how painful laminitis/founder is to a horse!

A look inside the hoof

The horse's foot is basically a specially adapted version of your fingernail or toenail. The hard, outer layer is "dead" tissue — with no direct nerve or blood supply, like the part of your nails that you periodically clip off. The hoof grows downward from the coronary band, the equivalent of your nail "root." With the exception of the part of the hoof closest to the ground or shoe, the insensitive, "dead" outer hoof wall is firmly attached to the sensitive, live tissues underneath. These attaching tissues are called the laminae and function like your nail bed. If the horse's hoof was thin and transparent, like your nails, you would see the same pink tissue underneath it.

Unlike a human nail, the horse's hoof wraps around the sides and back of his finger/digit. The pastern and foot of the horse contain the same bones as the distal end of your finger. The coffin joint, which sits just below the level of the horse's coronary band, is the same joint as your last knuckle.

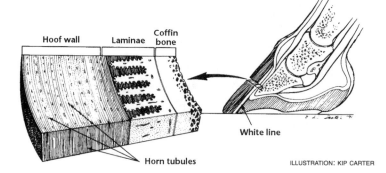

ILLUSTRATION: KIP CARTER

When a horse founders

There are still many gaps in our understanding of how laminitis happens, but the basic sequence of events goes like this:

■ **Phase one involves a restriction in blood flow to the feet** (except in the case of road founder). This can have different causes, but the result is the same. The tissues inside the foot do not receive enough oxygen, and some of the cells of the laminae begin to die. This loosens the "grip" of the laminae on the outer hoof wall. At this stage of laminitis, the horse will probably not show any lameness. If you feel his hooves, however, they will be icy cold.

If you get migraine headaches, you are familiar with the initial stages, where there are visual disturbances and spots or triangles before your eyes. This is similar to what is going on in the vaso-constrictive (blood shut-off) phase of laminitis. You don't have a headache yet, but you know that when your vision clears, you will.

■ **In phase two of laminitis (or a migraine headache), the blood flow returns to the area where it had been shut down — often with extreme force.** Your migraine will be pounding, as will the pulses in the back of the horse's ankle, along the arteries that feed the foot. His feet will have the characteristic hot feeling to the touch at this point, and the horse will be lame. This is the stage where most horses are diagnosed.

Inside the hoof, several things occur. Tiny clots may be present in many of the smaller arteries, blocking blood flow and triggering reflexes that raise blood pressure inside the foot even further, in an attempt to force blood through. This causes more pain. Blood vessels that were damaged during the phase of decreased blood flow or are under the influence of toxins or chemicals leak out more fluid than they normally would. Tissue damage in the laminae that occurred as a result of decreased blood flow triggers inflammatory responses, and this also makes fluid leak out of the blood vessels. The result is a collection of blood and/or fluids from the blood inside the hoof wall sandwiched between the outer layers of hoof wall and the laminae — much like that ugly purple bruise you get under your fingernail if you injure it.

Rotation

When people talk about a horse having foundered, one of the first things they want to know is, "Did he rotate?" **Rotation refers to** movement of the coffin bone (the third phalanx or "P3") inside the hoof wall. In a normal foot, the hoof wall and interconnections with the laminae suspend the coffin bone in a position where the edge of the bone, viewing the hoof from the side, is perfectly parallel to the edge of the hoof wall.

In laminitis, when the laminae are torn or weakened and fluid collects between the hoof wall and the laminae, the pressure can force the coffin bone away from its parallel position, so that the tip of the bone begins to point down toward the sole. **The downward rotation of the tip of the coffin bone is caused by the pull of the deep flexor tendon, which attaches to it.**

If a large number of the laminae have ruptured, the coffin bone will also sink down toward the sole, which is associated with the development of a deep indentation at the coronary band. This is very bad news for the horse. When rotation is severe, the pressure from the bone can actually cause the coffin bone to poke through the bottom of the sole. It doesn't take much imagination to understand the pain or severity of this condition.

Founder or laminitis

Some authors make a distinction between "founder" and "laminitis." For practical purposes, it's the same condition, with founder more of a layman's term and laminitis a medical term.

Specific causes of founder/laminitis

Septicemia/toxemia: **Septicemia means bacteria is in the blood. Toxemia is the presence in the blood of toxins produced by bacteria.** In most cases, this occurs when there is either a pathogenic (disease-causing/"bad") bacteria growing inside the intestinal tract, such as salmonella, or if there has been a sudden upset in the balance of organisms inside the intestinal tract (usually caused by a sudden diet change), horse accidentally getting into grain (grain overload) or use of oral (possibly intravenous) antibiotics. Several things happen in these situations that can contribute to founder.

There will often be large fluid shifts — fluid being pumped into the intestinal tract — that can lower blood pressure and cause the body to reflexively decrease blood flow to noncritical areas, including the feet. Blood-clotting abnormalities can develop, leading

Check the temperature of your horse's feet as a regular part of daily care.

to the formation of tiny blood clots in the small vessels throughout the body, including the feet. The inflamed intestinal tract may let many materials be absorbed into the blood stream that it would normally keep out. This is called a "leaky-gut syndrome." The foreign material is treated as an invader by the body and triggers an inflammatory and, often, an allergic reaction. Histamine and other substances produced by activated white blood cells may also cause the blood vessels to the feet to contract.

Another common cause is a retained placenta. This occurs when a mare has foaled but has not expelled all of the membranes from the pregnancy from her uterus. After foaling, any retained blood and tissue is a perfect place for bacteria to breed. Serious illness usually results in 24 hours or so, and laminitis results in nearly all these mares.

Grass founder: Grass founder is a poorly understood problem that usually affects ponies, but horses are susceptible as well. Grass founder occurs when some ponies (or horses) are allowed unrestricted access to lush pastures. This predominantly occurs in the spring, but areas that experience a rapid regrowth in cooler fall weather (southern states) may see problems at this time as well.

Many possibilities have been suggested as a cause for grass founder, some quite reasonable and others far-fetched. It has even been suggested that higher estrogen levels in young plants may cause this (although there is no proof for that claim nor is it rational). Magnesium deficiency has been suggested as a cause, since this is sometimes associated with founder in cattle under similar circumstances. The proposed treatment/cure/preventative is high doses of magnesium sulfate — Epsom salts.

Probably the most rational explanation for grass founder is some type of intestinal imbalance from the "rich diet" change, with a disruption of the normal intestinal flora and resultant toxemia or "leaky-gut syndrome." If Epsom salts do help, it may be more likely that this is because they are essentially flushing out the intestinal tract (they are used for constipation and stimulate the gut), not because of the magnesium content.

The higher protein content of young grasses has been suspected as a cause, but there is no good explanation for this. A more likely factor is the lower fiber and higher digestible carbohydrate in young grasses. The metabolism of a pony is designed for survival on sparse vegetation of poor quality, not unlimited succulent grasses.

Drug-induced founder: Corticosteroids (drugs such as dexamethasone or Azium, cortisone, flumethasone, beta-methasone) are often implicated as a cause of laminitis. These drugs have powerful effects on the metabolism of cells, in addition to their anti-inflammatory effects, and this may be how they result in laminitis. Laminitis from corticosteroids usually results when the drugs have been injected into the vein or a muscle or were added to the feed. Less commonly, injections for cosmetic reasons (i.e., into a splint or a capped hock, curb, etc.), injections to treat inflamed tendons or injections into joints for arthritis have been suspected of causing laminitis.

The corticosteroids prednisone and prednisolone are considered to have the least risk of causing laminitis, while strong anti-inflammatory steroids like betamethasone or flumethasone have the highest risk. Many veterinarians prefer to use prednisone or prednisolone for this reason.

Road founder

Road founder occurs in a horse who does not have any disease or upset in another part of his body causing the laminitis, except overwork and excessive pounding on a hard surface. (Road founder got its name because it was recognized in horses who had been worked for long distances on the road.) If you walk, run or hike for too long, your feet will become hot, swollen and painful. The same thing happens to the inside of the horse's hoof with one distinction — he can't pull off his shoes. The inflammation is trapped inside the hoof wall with no place for the pressure to go. In some cases, there may also be an actual shearing and tearing apart of the laminae from the hoof wall. The physical trauma combined with accumulation of fluids inside the foot, caused by inflammation making the blood vessels "leaky," results in laminitis.

Treatment of laminitis

Successful treatment begins with early detection. As we said, the sequence of events that result in damage begins long before the horse becomes lame. **Check the temperature of your horse's feet every day, morning and night, by reaching down and placing the palm of your hand across the front of the hoof.** Normal temperatures range from cool to slightly warm. **All four feet should feel the same.**

If your horse is showing any signs of illness (depressed, off feed, especially if colicky, has diarrhea, etc.), checking the feet should be routine, as should taking a temperature. If you detect or suspect any significant change in the temperature of the feet, whether the horse is lame or not, consult the veterinarian immediately. Drugs such as antihistamines and anti-inflammatories may head off a serious laminitis problem if administered quickly enough.

In cases of grain overload, it is important to get the veterinarian to the barn as soon as possible to treat the horse with large amounts of mineral oil, to coat the intestine and move the offending grain through quicker, and usually sodium bicarbonate to correct the acid condition of the intestine. Activated charcoal may also be used, especially in diarrhea cases, to absorb toxins. Bismuth subsalicylate (Pepto-Bismol) is another good toxin-absorbing treatment.

When a bacterial infection is also involved (septicemia/toxemia), specific treatment for the problem is also indicated. Another thing the vet may do is inject local anesthetic ("nerve block") along the nerves and blood vessels supplying the feet. The local anesthetic will relieve pain and also relieve any spasm in the blood vessels supplying the feet. Blood flow seems to return more to normal levels — neither excessively high nor low.

The day-to-day and hour-to-hour care of the foundered horse will be your responsibility. If you listen to enough different people, you are sure to get advice

Keep horses out of the feed room and grain bins securely closed.

that is directly contradictory. Do you walk them or not? Hot-water treatment or cold? Packing the feet or not packing the feet? We will go into these in detail. Before that, though, just let one important principle be burned into your memory — USE COMMON SENSE!

Walking a foundered horse is a hotly debated issue. Some claim you must walk them to restore the blood flow. Others caution that walking encourages rotation of the coffin bone, which is what we believe. **A horse who is rooted to the spot or lying down, pulse elevated, blowing in pain, possibly sweating, is telling you that he should not be moved.** A tremendous amount of weight is placed on the feet with each step. Movement may further rupture weakened attachments between the hoof wall and laminae, encouraging rotation. Damaged blood vessels may also tear or rupture. Walking will not remove clots from the circulation or cause spasmed blood vessels to relax. **Bottom line: Do not force acutely foundered horses to walk.**

Hot vs. cold water is also controversial. Hot advocates try to encourage blood flow; cold supporters want to cut inflammation and pain. Common sense prevails again.

Cold water should be used if the hoof is hot. This usually means for the first three days to two weeks or so following a bout of laminitis, the goal must be to control and eliminate inflammation so healing can begin. Once the horse has completely stabilized (or if you are lucky enough to catch the problem early on, **when the feet are frigidly cold), hot/warm water will encourage additional blood flow and speed healing.**

Packing the feet is another area where rational thought shows the way. Packing with hard materials is not advisable, since it will put excessive pressure on the sole. This not only causes pain; it may also injure the tissues trapped between the sole and the point of the rotating coffin bone, possibly causing the bone to puncture through.

One rationale behind packing the foot was to prevent the coffin bone from rotation. However, the weight of the horse puts such a tremendous force on this bone there is nothing — short of preventing the horse from bearing weight — that can counteract that.

If coffin-bone rotation is not a threat, packing with softer materials (poultice, soft acrylic) may increase the horse's comfort. **Best of all is the old-fashioned remedy — stand the horse in a muddy stream bed!** The flowing water will cool the feet, while the soft stream bottom provides a cushioned floor. We know of veterinarians who give that advice to this day, often with good results.

If you do not have a running stream conveniently close by, another good alternative is Custom Support Foam available through 3M Animal Care Products, a product your farrier will apply. This material is soaked in water then positioned firmly using tape on the sole. It is soft enough to conform to the foot and provide a good cushion with gentle support for the coffin bone. It can be removed to examine the sole and simply replaced.

Feeding the foundered horse

When a horse has foundered, your feeding program must accommodate his decreased activity level and prevent harmful excessive weight by adjusting the calories he takes in. Equally important is to provide the horse with all the basic materials he needs to rebuild a strong and healthy hoof.

In terms of calories, you will rarely, if ever, need to worry about getting the horse to lose weight in the early stages. Laminitis is such a stressful situation that the pounds seem to melt off. This is usually complicated by a depressed appetite.

If horses continue to lose weight beyond the first week or two, addition of an energy-rich fat supplement is preferable to grain. We like CocoSoya from Uckele Animal Health, a blend of coconut and soy oil that smells like caramel and is highly palatable. Start at about one-half cup per day and work up to one to two cups, as needed. This is a natural oil with minimal processing that is stabilized by adding vitamin E. It contains a generous level of the essential fatty acids that are destroyed by the stabilization processes used to manufacture "store-bought" cooking vegetable oils. This can be sprayed on hay or soaked into hay cubes.

Your horse's basic diet should provide both high-quality protein (the hoof is 95 percent protein, so this is no time

to have the horse on a low total protein or poor-quality protein diet), a balance of minerals, high fiber for intestinal-tract health, and minimal to no grain.

There is no single type of hay that can meet these needs. The ideal hay would be about 50% alfalfa and 50% grass hay. Feed as much as the horse wants to eat, restricting only if obvious weight gain occurs. If good alfalfa hay is not available in your area, consider alfalfa cubes. These should be fed in the same amount, pound per pound, as hay.

If getting good grass hay is the problem, consider either a complete feed that is beet-pulp based or a mixed grass/alfalfa cube.

Your mixed-hay diet will be around 12% protein, most of it of adequate quality, but not enough for a horse under this degree of metabolic stress. We strongly recommend you also feed one to two pounds of a high-quality protein supplement. Inquire in feed and tack stores in your area. You want one that is at least 50% milk-protein based (or alfalfa-meal based).

Finally, you will need to feed a supplement designed to meet the needs of hooves. Some nutritionists even recommend you feed double to four times the level of biotin, methionine and zinc found in most supplements. We would suggest a minimum of 25 to 40 mg of biotin, 6 to 8 grams of methionine (your basic diet and protein supplement will help meet this need) and 250 to 350 mg of zinc in a chelated (protein-bound) form.

The role of the farrier

The farrier plays an extremely important, indispensable, part in the treatment of the foundered horse. Correct trimming and shoeing can make a difference in the horse's comfort within minutes and affect the ultimate outcome. Your shoer will be able to work the most effectively after X-rays are available. These will show the position of the coffin bone within the hoof and guide him in getting the correct angle to the foot.

A bar shoe distributes the horse's weight over a wider surface than regular shoes.

In the acute case (first 72 hours or so), shoes are pulled by removing nails carefully one at a time. The toe will be "snubbed" and rolled. If a large collection of blood/fluid is present inside the foot, the farrier and veterinarian may decide it is best to relieve some of this pressure by drilling holes in the hoof wall or removing a portion of the hoof wall at the toe to allow drainage. Drastic changes in heel length and angle will probably be avoided at this time unless there is something on the X-rays to indicate otherwise.

This will be a matter of professional judgment between the veterinarian and farrier, who must work closely. For example, if a horse has low heels to begin with, the pull of the deep flexor tendon will be extremely strong and could worsen rotation. It might be advisable in this case to raise the heels/angle of the foot slightly to decrease that pull.

In most cases, changes are postponed until the condition has stabilized. At that point, the most current X-rays will show how much rotation, if any, is present. The shoer will then remove as much toe as needed, or as much as possible, to attempt to line up the front of the coffin bone with the hoof wall. Lowering of the heels will be necessary to line up the bottom surface of the coffin bone with the sole. However, this must be done gradually and cautiously, since a dramatic lowering of the angles will increase the pull of the deep flexor tendon on the recently damaged laminae and may cause more rotation.

As a quick note on shoeing, there is no single shoe that is appropriate for all cases of laminitis. Shoe selection, like trimming, must be based on the position of the coffin bone within the foot, along with an educated guess as to where the strongest forces are operating on the coffin bone to move it out of position. Wide-webbed shoes, possibly some type of bar (type is critical) and possible use of a soft, resilient cushioning material are all possibilities, but the exact shoeing method will be chosen on an individual basis.

Preventing laminitis

Unfortunately, we may not always be able to prevent laminitis. However, we can avoid situations associated with laminitis and watch for early signs of laminitis, if the horse becomes ill or is otherwise at risk. You must be especially careful with a horse or pony who has foundered in the past, since the foot is somewhat weakened for the rest of his life, and this animal will always be at greater risk of laminitis.

To decrease the chance of laminitis:
■ Make gradual changes in feed.
■ Monitor grazing on lush spring pastures (especially ponies).
■ Avoid rapid increase in grain feeding — always store grain in containers that are "horse-proof."
■ Inspect placentas carefully after a mare has foaled, to make sure there are no pieces missing.
■ Use corticosteroids sparingly.
■ Make checking hoof temperature a part of daily grooming.
■ Avoid working a horse heavily or for prolonged time periods on hard ground or roads.
■ Be alert for early signs of laminitis in any horse who is ill or has a digestive system problem.

Complete regrowth of the hoof wall after laminitis will take about nine months. How comfortable your horse is during this time will be a function of the degree of laminitis and your farrier's skill. Regular X-rays will help guide corrective trimming. ▣

14

Get A Handle On HYPP

*If you own a Quarter Horse, or plan to,
you need to know that HYPP is more than a
few letters in a stallion advertisement.*

According to the American Quarter Horse Association, hyperkalemic periodic paralysis (HYPP) is "a muscular disease caused by a hereditary genetic defect that leads to uncontrolled muscle twitching or profound muscle weakness, and, in severe cases, may lead to collapse and/or death."

Researchers were able to locate the HYPP gene in horses rather quickly because, while rare, the same gene occurs in humans, causing identical symptoms. The involved gene controls the sodium-potassium pump, the "device" in the muscle cell that regulates the flow of sodium and potassium into and out of cells. Normal muscle cells have high levels of potassium and low levels of sodium.

In HYPP, too much sodium enters the cell and too much potassium leaves it, leading to hyperkalemia (high blood potassium). **It is low potassium inside muscle cells that causes attacks of muscle weakness, not the high potassium outside them. However, high blood potassium can and does cause rhythm abnormalities in the heart, and this is what leads to death in severe cases.** An attack can also occur if a horse eats a meal containing a large amount of potassium, making the control mechanisms in the muscle cells go "haywire."

Horses who carry two involved genes (homozygous) are designated HYPP (H/H). Horses who carry a single involved gene (heterozygous) are HYPP (N/H). Heterozygous horses are less severely affected, often having no apparent symptoms. It is speculated that some muscle spasms may occur unobserved.

Most horses afflicted with HYPP are heavily muscled.

Managing the disease

Careful feeding is essential to minimize the possibility of HYPP episodes. The goal is a diet that avoids intake of large amounts of potassium at any one time. However, potassium is essential for the function of all cells and must be maintained at low-normal levels.

By keeping the horse's blood potassium in the low-normal range, you establish a balance that should be able to withstand those inevitable times when the muscle cells put out too much potassium, hopefully without triggering an attack.

A diet of plain oats and grass hay (rather than alfalfa) provides the lowest level of potassium while maintaining good health. A vitamin-mineral supplement with no potassium may be added to the diet, as well as a plain white salt block. Never use electrolyte replacement products, even in hot weather, unless your veterinarian has specifically made a recommendation. Electrolytes contain concentrated amounts of potassium, as well as sodium.

Plenty of fresh water is necessary for any horse, but it's even more critical for horses with HYPP. Excess potassium circulating in the blood is pumped out in the urine. If the body's water level drops to lower than normal, the kidneys, which are sensitive to even a slight degree of dehydration will reduce their production of urine.

The drug acetazolamide (Diamox) often decreases the frequency and severity of attacks. Diamox prompts the kidneys to produce slightly more urine than normal, containing more potassium than normal. Diamox also can slow the uptake of potassium by cells, protecting the heart from an overload of potassium. Unfortunately, that can also worsen the weakness caused by low potassium inside muscle cells. For this reason, Diamox is not always the best thing to use when a horse is showing symptoms. However, the overall effect of lowering total body potassium makes it beneficial in the day-to-day maintenance of horses with HYPP.

Other drugs (i.e. metaproteronol, propanolol, triampterene) are being studied for use in horses. Some may prove to be more effective than Diamox. If you have an HYPP horse and Diamox is not working as well as hoped, contact your closest veterinary school for referral to a researcher who may be able to help you.

Diamox is a forbidden substance at shows sanctioned by both the AQHA and AHSA.

HYPP and diet

Most owners of HYPP horses know to avoid alfalfa hay because it is a rich potassium source. However, some grass hays aren't much better. Early cutting, good-quality timothy may have a potassium level of around 2% (similar to alfalfa), as can orchard grass hay. Even Bermuda grass hay can have a potassium level as high as 1.9%.

If your veterinarian cautions that the potassium level in the diet is of critical importance in your horse's case, investigate beet pulp as part of your roughage source. Beet pulp's potassium content is extremely low at 0.2%.

Stick to plain grains rather than complete feeds or commercial sweet feeds. Molasses is very high at 2.98%, while the soybean and alfalfa meals (often used as a base or to adjust protein content) average around 2% potassium. Wheat bran, at 1.22%, is lower than rice bran at 1.71%.

Panola grass hay and peanut hay have the lowest potassium content in the NRC's tables. However, a good rule of thumb is that any hay cut in early growth stages will contain more potassium, even more than midbloom-to-late alfalfa hays. Pasture is your best option, as the high moisture content dilutes potassium down to 0.5% or less. You can make up for a plain diet by liberal treats of carrots. At 0.32% potassium, carrots are a good choice for the HYPP horse.

The role of exercise

When a muscle is signaled to work, the sodium-potassium pump moves potassium out of the cell and lets sodium in. When the cell has finished its work, the pump works in reverse, letting potassium back in and sodium out. It is this second step, the uptake of potassium by the muscle cell, that benefits horses with HYPP.

So, sometimes it is possible to abort an attack of HYPP by forcing the horse to work — work signals his muscles to do the sodium-potassium swap. This may also be why turnout with unrestricted movement/exercise is of benefit to HYPP horses. Horses with HYPP do well in an open stall-paddock arrangement.

Sometimes horses have an attack during cool-down, 45 minutes to three hours after work. Often these attacks go unnoticed. Here's what happens: During and right after exercise, the muscle cells release more potassium than normal. The red blood cells and other tissues help to soak up this excess. But then, about an hour and a half after exercise has stopped, all the cells redistribute the potassium in attempts to get back to normal levels. The red blood cells dump potassium abck into the blood. And, the result is the same as if the horse ate a high-potassium meal — an attack can be triggered.

What to do during an HYPP episode

An episode can be recognized by muscle twitching, tremors or spasms, and the horse may appear weak and stumble. The symptoms can vary widely from horse to horse. If you are riding, get off and remove the saddle. Hand walk or lunge the horse in a safe place with soft footing, like grass or an arena. The exercise can encourage reuptake of potassium from the blood by the muscles.

Raising the blood sugar level will cause the potassium to go inside the muscle cells where it belongs and reduce weakness. In fact, emergency treatment of an HYPP episode always involves the administration of concentrated sugar solutions directly into the vein.

If your horse is not having difficulty breathing or swallowing, feed grain (oats, corn or barley), or Karo syrup for glucose, which promotes the uptake of potassium. You can also try giving the horse one or two ounces of molasses or honey by dose syringe. Both of these substances are absorbed quickly and will give a rapid rise in blood sugar. Do not attempt therapy with feed or any oral substance unless you are certain breathing and swallowing are normal.

HYPP attacks can affect breathing and swallowing. If the horse is making an abnormal breathing noise, do not attempt to feed or water him. If his throat is not working properly, the food or water may end up in his lungs. If he is breathing normally, check for the ability to swallow by squirting

This Impressive-bred horse has characteristic good conformation.

a small amount of clean water into his mouth or just putting your finger in the side of the mouth in the gap between his teeth where the bit normally sits. This will stimulate the tongue to move and should induce the horse to swallow.

Administer Diamox if you have it on hand, but only by a veterinarian's instructions (Diamox during an attack could make the weakness worse). In a severe attack, when the horse is down and unable to stand, immediate veterinary attention is necessary. Weakness of the diaphragm and other muscles of breathing, as well as high blood potassium causing abnormalities in the heart, could be life-threatening.

Breeding horses with HYPP

The AQHA does not restrict the breeding or registration of horses having HYPP (H/H) or (N/H). However, testing is required for recent foals descending from Impressive, and registration certificates will be issued showing the horse's HYPP status. (For more information see the AQHA's Official Handbook, Rule 205.)

Careful consideration should be given to avoiding the propagation of this disease. As stated, the symptoms vary widely, and while a sire or dam may be asymptomatic, a foal could be severely affected. Homozygous horses will pass on the disease 100 percent of the time, while heterozygous horses will pass it on 50 percent, even when bred to a normal horse. The only way to eradicate this disease entirely is to refrain from breeding any horse carrying the gene.

What it all means

With proper management, horses afflicted with HYPP can be perfectly usable and long-lived. However, restrictions and/or medication requirements may limit the activities the horse is expected to do. The more owners and potential buyers know, the less likely their horses will experience uncomfortable and sometimes painful attacks.

For more information, call the AQHA at 1-800-414-RIDE and ask for the HYPP brochure.

Valerie's story

Valerie Harrison, a Perfect Horse *reader, found out first-hand about HYPP and shared her experience with us:*
Six months ago, I purchased a Quarter Horse broodmare. After the check was written and the horse loaded, the seller leaned in my truck window and asked, "Do you know anything about HYPP?" I replied, "Uh...It's kinda like tying up, isn't it? Why do you ask?" She replied, "Well, this mare's a negative/positive. That means if you breed her, you need to choose a negative/negative stud." I thanked her, saying "That shouldn't be a problem."

I appreciated the seller passing on this bit of information. In my ignorance, I assumed that HYPP was only an important factor in choosing a potential stallion. I certainly didn't realize that it was a potentially fatal disease exclusive to descendants of the Quarter Horse sire Impressive. Heck, at that point I didn't even realize that my new mare, Obvious Conclusion, was a descendant of Impressive.

After I'd had the mare awhile, I talked with owners of other negative/positive mares. They set my mind at ease for awhile, but now it seems I wasn't the only misinformed Quarter Horse owner around.

Recently at the end of a short ride, I noticed my mare twitching and stumbling. The long muscle along her throat was undulating, and I felt tremors along her barrel and flanks. I got off and removed the saddle. I panicked and called the vet.

Vet: Is this your first experience with HYPP?

Me: But she doesn't have HYPP!

Valerie's beautiful Obvious Conclusion mare.

Vet: Hmmmm... Do you have her test results?

Me: Well, no. But I can get them.

I didn't mention the single positive I'd been told about, because I honestly thought it was unimportant. No wonder the vet was concerned. I thought maybe I'd been suckered, but when I called the previous owner, she'd already told me all she knew, but gave me the specifics of my mare's test result.

Armed with that little bit of information and the mare's history, I called the vet back. I discovered that I had been given a common misinterpretation of the "negative/positive" result. It turned out that my horse did indeed have HYPP and had exhibited classic symptoms of the disease. The vet strongly discouraged me from ever breeding her but couldn't answer my questions as to her future usability. It seems that the degree of symptoms varies widely in horses who are heterozygous (one normal, one positive gene).

I set out to learn all I could about HYPP. I found there were many factors that may have been involved in the attack that day — after years of little or no work, we'd had an intense training session, then the horse had been left overnight in an unfamiliar place and fed hay she wasn't used to. I found out the episodes can be brought on by stress, such as she experienced, or can occur at random. My mare could have been having these attacks all along, since she was ridden infrequently.

Testing for HYPP

Testing is performed at the University of California at Davis. The test requires the horseowner to pull approximately 50 hairs (including roots) from the horse's mane or tail and send them next-day air, along with a check for $35 (payable to U.C. Regents) and the horse's name and registration number as recorded on his papers.

Veterinary Genetics Laboratory — HYPP Testing
Old Davis Road
University of California
Davis, CA 95616-8744
916-752-9780
FAX 916-752-3556 ■PH■

15

The Rabies Threat: Not Worth The Gamble!

Rabies is untreatable and almost always fatal. Vaccinating your animals offers the safest protection for both man and beast.

Rabies is a viral disease of the central nervous system. The vast majority of cases are caused by the bite of a rabid animal (virus is present in large amounts in the saliva). Although it is rare, transmission may occur through contamination of an open wound (i.e., to a human with a cut on their hand who is examining the mouth of a rabid animal) or even by inhalation. (Transmission has been known to occur by breathing the air in bat caves inhabited by large numbers of rabid bats).

The virus travels along the nerves in the area of the bite, enters the spinal cord and finally the brain. However, the spread along the nerves does not occur until after the virus has multiplied for approximately five days in the local area of the bite. Since the virus is never found in the salivary glands before it has invaded the brain, it is believed to travel from the brain to the salivary glands via their nerve supply.

The raccoon, skunk and bat are among the most often identified carriers of rabies that come in contact with man and domestic animals.

Time between infection and development of clinical symptoms (incubation period) is usually in the neighborhood of 15 to 50 days. Bites in the head and neck will result in signs appearing more quickly than bites on the extremities, since the distance to the brain is shorter. In rare cases, incubation periods may stretch to months or even years.

Who is affected?

All warm-blooded animals are susceptible to the rabies virus. The disease is endemic in bats, skunks, raccoons and foxes. There are different strains of the virus that may cause different symptoms, but "species specific" strains can easily cause rabies in another species and may result in infection that permits the host to live for longer-than-normal periods. For example, some bats may be actively infected, yet survive for months or years when the infecting virus is "bat specific."

Clinical signs

The symptoms of rabies are divided into three stages: the prodromal phase, the excitative (or dumb) phase, and the terminal paralytic phase.

In the prodromal stage, animals may or may not have a fever. They commonly stop eating or drinking and may be reclusive. Inability to retain saliva (which causes foaming at the mouth) may develop at this time, but this is not a constant finding.

Behavior changes occur in the second phase. The excitative or furious form of rabies is characterized by extreme alertness, roaming into unusual locations, loss of fear of man or natural enemies, and marked aggression. Dogs bite at the slightest provocation and will attack any moving object, including cars. Cats attack, inflicting extensive scratches and bites. Cows become increasingly vocal, with a bellow that is said to be characteristic and never forgotten once you have heard it. Cows will also attack, charging any moving object. Since cows have no upper teeth, they are not likely to inflict a significant bite. However, an enraged cow can still easily maim or kill.

The dumb form of rabies is the most commonly observed in horses and cattle, although it can occur in any animal. Depression is a characteristic symptom of this form of infection. Inability to swallow saliva develops early in the course of the disease, along

A horse with rabies is more likely to be depressed than aggressive.

with a slack jaw. Paralysis accompanied by an abnormal gait and the eventual inability to rise are also seen, as the disease progresses to coma and death. **It is important to note that rabies in horses can easily be confused with other problems, including a foreign body in the mouth.** If a person has any areas of broken skin on their hands or forearms, they might easily become infected when examining the mouth of an infected horse. Rabies in horses may also be confused with a variety of neurological problems including botulism, equine protozoal myeoencephalitis (EPM), head injury, spinal cord injury or a viral encephalomyelitis.

In the final stages, animals are recumbent, become progressively paralyzed, enter a coma and die.

There are a few rare cases where people or animals have recovered from rabies. However, the vast majority of cases are fatal.

Who has the problem

Rabies virus occurs virtually worldwide, the only exceptions being countries that have taken extreme measures to eradicate the disease (such as Great Britain).

Because rabies is easily confused with other, more common neurological diseases, the numbers may be deceptively low. Diagnosis is also somewhat difficult, since it requires that the head/brain be delivered rapidly and intact to an appropriately equipped diagnostic laboratory for study. In fact, it is possible that all large animal domestic cases are either under-diagnosed and/or under-reported.

Not all cases of rabies in horses have been typed as to the species of the virus. However, we do know that some cases were traced to the bat virus, and still others were likely of raccoon origin.

The dramatic rise in reported cases of wild animal rabies in the United States is especially alarming. This is particularly true since these numbers obviously are not representative of the total number of rabies cases in wild animals. How many others may have died unnoticed in the woods or killed by cars? **As the population of rabid wild animals increases, so does the risk of infection for domestic animals and man.**

Cats and dogs are at greatest risk for infection because of their tendency to wander freely into the natural habitat of the wild animals carrying rabies. Stabled and pastured animals are at less risk of encountering a rabid animal, but the chances will steadily rise as the number of rabid wild animals rises. Rabid animals have also been seen to walk boldly right into a barn. Rabies has even been diagnosed in horses strictly confined to their stalls on race courses. Every building potentially harbors bats.

Rabies is endemic (always present) throughout the United States. Epidemic (uncontrolled rise) conditions exist along the east coast, from Florida to Maine and inland to Tennessee, where the problem animals vary from raccoons to skunks in any given year. California is experiencing a severe problem with skunk rabies, while Texas is in the throes of an epidemic with wild animal sources, which include the coyote, grey fox and skunk.

There is currently no effective blood test for rabies.

Three rabid horses: The threat is real

While the number of cases confirmed in horses is small, the true picture is scary.

A raccoon was seen to attack a pony in a pasture, and the pony was bitten. The raccoon was killed and determined to be positive for rabies. The owners had the pony euthanized rather than risk exposure to their children.

A horse died unexpectedly. The attending veterinarian sent tissue and blood samples to the lab to establish the cause of death. The tests came back positive for rabies. The owners and all persons having recent contact with that horse had to undergo post-exposure treatment.

A horse died having a tentative diagnosis of Eastern equine encephalitis. Tissues were sent to the National Veterinary Diagnostic Lab, who determined he did not have EEE but had rabies. All persons having contact with the horse or its infectious tissues were evaluated for exposure and treated as necessary.

Prevention

Attempts to control wild animal sources of rabies are expensive and largely futile — the problem is simply far too widespread. **It is universally agreed that the best approach to limiting rabies in all domestic species is through vaccination.**

Horse owners are generally pretty responsible about vaccinating their dogs, but barn cats are another concern, as are any other pets, including horses, llamas and pot-bellied pigs. **If your animal has significant economic or emotional value to you, or if that animal could put you at risk for contracting rabies, it should be vaccinated.**

Because of the seriousness of the disease, farriers, veterinarians and anyone handling wildlife or livestock with significant exposure to possibly rabid animals should also be vaccinated. Though there is no treatment for rabies and since infection is almost always fatal, vaccination provides strong protection.

The enemy?

Today, the only natural enemy of the raccoon is man, and ironically, it is man who also feeds him. In years past, raccoons had to rely on a diet of berries, insects and frogs. With the spread of housing and farmland into what used to be forests, raccoons now dine on an assortment of apples, corn, vegetables from the garden, pet food and anything they can scrounge from our trash cans. Because of their cute face, children are often attracted to raccoons, but should be warned that the raccoon's mask could hide a deadly threat.

What to do if a person or an animal is bitten or exposed

1. Wash the wound thoroughly with soap and water. The rabies virus has a sheath of fat around it. Washing with soap and water dissolves this sheath, causing the virus to break apart.

2. Contact your physician immediately to consider post-exposure treatment and a tetanus booster.

Regarding the potentially rabid animal:
■ *If it is a pet or livestock, carefully capture and confine the animal. Report the incident immediately to the health department.*

■ *If it is a wild animal, kill the animal if possible, without damaging its head. Wearing rubber gloves, place the carcass in a plastic bag and put it in a cool (not freezing) location. Immediately contact a health department official.*

A bite by a potentially rabid animal is nothing to "wait and see" about. Immediate action may save a life. ■PH■

16

Chronic Respiratory Problems

*Does your horse have a persistent cough,
nasal discharge or noisy breathing?
Don't despair. In many cases, good management
and watchful care can help your horse breathe easier.*

When you blow into a musical instrument or even an empty paper-towel roll, the sound produced varies with how hard you blow, how long you maintain the flow of air and even the way you hold your lips or the shape and diameter of the instrument. Similarly, normal variations in the horse's head, throat, nasal passages and nostrils can influence the sound you hear when he is breathing. The sounds most horses make when they breathe hard differs from the sounds they make when breathing quietly at rest. Most of the time this is normal and caused by the turbulence produced when moving large amounts of air at a rapid rate.

Abnormal breathing sounds are usually louder than normal. However, "loud breathing" itself may be perfectly normal for your horse. To determine whether it's normal or an indication of a problem, ask your veterinarian to examine the horse.

Whistling and fluttering are two of the most common abnormal breathing sounds. To an experienced veterinarian, the character of the sound and the phase of respiration when it occurs (when the horse is inhaling, exhaling or both) will often be enough to come to a likely diagnosis. **Diagnosis is confirmed by physical examination and palpation of the head and throat, followed by endoscopy — the passage of a "scope" into the horse's nose and throat area to look at the anatomy.**

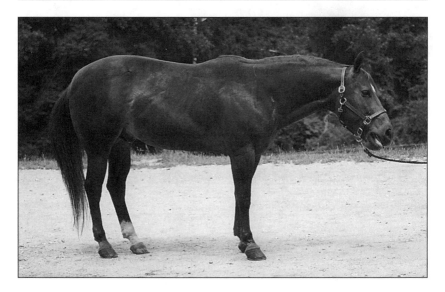

A horse with chronic cough or respiratory problems may have a full-time job getting enough air. His abdominal muscles are often well developed and his nostrils flared.

Some anatomic abnormalities are more annoying than functionally significant. This includes problems like excessive alar folds (a large amount of tissue and/or deeper-than-normal cavity in the blind pouch that sits back inside the horse's nostril) or deformities of the nasal septum, the structure that divides the nose and nasal passage into right and left sides.

Noises originating in the throat are potentially more serious, as they indicate interference with the normal flow of air. "Roaring" is caused by paralysis of the muscles that open and close the entry to the airway during breathing. Various abnormalities of the soft palate and nearby structures inside the throat can also interfere with breathing and result in an abnormal noise. Generally, these are of more significance to horses who perform at speed than to horses involved in less strenuous activities. Surgical correction may be an option.

Stable cough

The term "stable cough" refers to horses who have a dry, persistent cough whenever they are in the barn. There is no fever or nasal discharge associated with the cough, and the horse will usually otherwise appear completely normal — normal appetite and so forth. There is usually no obvious decrease in the horse's ability to tolerate exercise, although heavy exercise at speed may also cause the horse to cough for a short period after exercise.

Causes: Stable cough is caused by an increased sensitivity to the many, many potential irritants found inside the barn/stall. This may be in the form of an overly sensitive/reactive upper airway or a true allergy. Ammonia (from urine breakdown), dust, microscopic organisms inside the dust (i.e., dust mites), molds and sensitivity to hay, straw or even a particular grain can be the cause. Poor ventilation, of course, makes the problem decidedly worse.

Treatment: Treatment involves controlling the sensitivity and eliminating the cause. Keeping the horse turned out will usually either greatly decrease or eliminate the coughing. Regardless of whether there is a true allergy or not, the cough is basically mediated by inflammation. Corticosteroids stop it temporarily but have serious side effects when used long-term. Plus, the problem returns when they are stopped.

Many horses respond well to measures to strengthen their immune response and get the cough under control at the same time. Antioxidants should be used on a daily basis, allowing three to six weeks for full effect. **Most important is vitamin C, as it plays the major role in the health of the respiratory system.** Feed at least 7.5 grams a day to start, decreasing the dose to a minimum of 4 to 4.5 grams a day once the horse begins to respond. Also effective are the bioflavinoids, cofactors for vitamin C, and the antioxidant grape-seed extract.

There is a delicate balance between a healthy immune system and inflammatory control systems that keep the immune reaction in check. You can help tip that balance in favor of controlled immune reactions by supplementing with essential fatty acids. Vegetable oils, such as linseed oil, flax-seed oil and soybean oil, are excellent sources of essential fatty acids and should be fed at one to three ounces per day, depending on size of the horse.

The herbal cough medication **Cough Free** is also helpful for many horses with stable cough. Unfortunately, like most herbal products, the horse may find the herbal smell too strong for his liking. You may be able to overcome any reluctance to eat it by mixing the herbal powder in your oil and then blending this crumb-like mixture into the grain well. Oils with a pleasant, appealing and strong odor/taste work best. We like **CocoSoya** by Uckele Health and Nutrition.

Do not waste your time on cough syrups to treat stable cough. Although many are temporarily effective, they do nothing to address the root of the problem, and the effect lasts a short time. For horses whose cough becomes worse with exercise, you can try a mentholated product such as **Hawthorne's Wind Aid** (liquid) or Uckele's **Respun Paste**. These work like a mentholated cough drop to temporarily quiet cough and ease breathing. Both of these products are effective, although the Respun has a less offensive odor and taste and contains other natural ingredients such as clove that are also helpful.

The main thrust in eliminating stable cough must be to remove the offending irritant. If an allergic reaction is involved, skin testing or blood testing for antibodies to allergens may provide the answer. However, more often than not, it is either not helpful or identifies so many possible problem substances that you would end up taking the same control measures as you would without knowing the test results.

Step one is to keep the horse outside as much as possible, which gives his throat a chance to quiet down without being bombarded by irritants. Make sure the barn is well ventilated, even in winter, when the horse is inside. Just because a closed-up barn still feels cool or cold in the winter does not mean there is good ventilation going through it.

Switch from straw to sawdust or wood shavings for bedding. Many irritants can be found in straw, from dust to microscopic molds. The horse's hay should be thoroughly shaken apart and doused in a bucket of water before feeding it. This settles dust particles and loose bits of hay that may be irritating.

The role of grain is sometimes harder to determine. The horse may cough more while eating grain either because of sensitivity to a specific component (chaff, soybean, alfalfa meal, etc.) or just because the grain physically irritates his throat. Feeding only triple-cleaned/screened, steamed and crimped "racehorse" oats is the best choice if grain is suspected to be contributing to the problem.

Gutteral-pouch infections and chronic nasal discharge

The gutteral pouches are air-filled sacs located along the sides of the throat, just behind the angle of the jaw. They open into the upper throat through two slit-like openings that are visible with an endoscope.

Because the gutteral pouch is in close proximity to the infected tissues of a horse with a strangles infection, if an infection gains access to this area, swelling will occur along the back edge of the jaw bone, giving the horse's head a blown-up appearance.

Classically, a horse with gutteral-pouch infection will have a thick, white-yellow nasal discharge on one side only — the side where the gutteral pouch is infected. Irritation of the throat from the drainage may cause a cough, but coughing is not usually a major problem. If large amounts of pus are trapped in the pouch, swelling may occur behind the jaw bone, from just below the base of the ear down to the throat level.

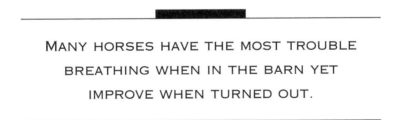

MANY HORSES HAVE THE MOST TROUBLE BREATHING WHEN IN THE BARN YET IMPROVE WHEN TURNED OUT.

Causes: Chronic gutteral-pouch infections may be bacterial or fungal. Fungal is particularly dangerous, since these organisms may invade deeply into the walls of the gutteral pouch and damage the blood vessels and nerves.

Treatment: Because there are important arterial and nervous structures lying close to the gutteral pouches, the veterinarian will probably use an endoscope and pass catheters/tubes inside the gutteral pouches to flush them out and infuse medications. These tubes may be left in place to provide an avenue of drainage and allow further treatments. Intramuscular or intravenous antibiotics and/or antifungals may also be recommended.

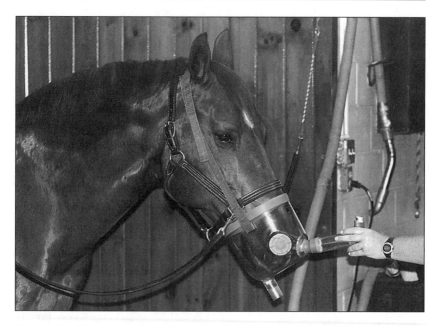

Since the horse won't voluntarily inhale any medication, devices have been developed to hold medication and force him to take a deep breath.

Allergic lung disease

The symptoms of allergic lung disease in horses are similar to those of asthma in people. They include wheezing, difficulty breathing, elevated breathing rate, decreased exercise tolerance and cough. In the early stages, these problems have a waxing and waning character, with the horse being fairly normal at times and at other times having "attacks" of breathing problems.

If left untreated, the lungs may become permanently damaged, giving the horse the equivalent of emphysema in people. In these late stages, the problems are often referred to as "heaves" — to describe how the horse's sides heave when he is fighting to get enough air.

Many horses have the most trouble breathing when in the barn, improving on turnout. Ability to exercise is greatly decreased. The human term for this disease, COPD or chronic obstructive pulmonary disease, is being used more and more to describe the equivalent in horses also.

The disease makes it difficult for the horse to empty the air from his lungs so that they can be refilled with clean, oxygen-rich air. He will use his abdominal muscles and the muscles between the ribs forcefully in trying to get the air out (normal breathing does not involve use of these muscles). His nostrils will flare with each breath, and the lining of the nose may appear more red than normal. **Respiratory rate (breaths per minute) will climb from the normal of about eight into the high teens or 20s.**

Causes: The common triggers of allergic respiratory problems in horses are the same as for stable cough (see page 162). In addition, there may be a seasonal pattern to allergic lung disease, related to flowering trees or plants, even fresh grass. **Horses kept in urban/industrial areas may also suffer the same lung problems from fumes and gases, as people do.**

Treatment: The treatment of an acute attack of COPD should always involve the veterinarian. Rapid control is important to make the horse more comfortable and to reduce strain on the lungs that could lead to irreversible damage. The veterinarian will usually use corticosteroids intravenously, then orally or by intramuscular injection. These both block the allergic response and cut inflammation. Antibiotics may be used initially, as well, to provide some protection against infection when on corticosteroids. A side effect of corticosteroids is a temporarily depressed immune response, leaving the horse more susceptible to infections.

Other medications can help the airways dilate, or open up. Atropine is effective, but it lasts a relatively short time. Epinephrine ("adrenalin") is also effective but has many side effects, such as elevated heart rate and jumpiness. The related chemical ephedrine lasts longer and has a somewhat lower incidence of side effects. Bronchodilators, such as albuterol or clenbuterol, help the muscles around the airways in the lung relax to allow more air into the lung. One of these drugs will often be prescribed for use for several weeks after an acute attack has been controlled. The horse may be able to be tapered off ("weaned" from) these drugs after a period of time.

As with stable cough, skin testing or blood allergy testing may identify offending irritants in the environment. This is more important to do with COPD than for stable cough, since repeated exposure leads to repeated attacks and eventual lung damage. Once the allergens are identified, steps can be taken to eliminate/minimize exposure, and the horse may also receive a series of desensitizing injections — "allergy shots."

The same antioxidant/anti-inflammatory nutrition support described for stable cough should also be used for horses with COPD. Correct nutritional and/or supplement use can dramatically decrease the need for prescription medications and make attacks less frequent. ▣

17

Strangling Strangles

If you have ever read the book or seen the movie "The Red Pony," you have a graphic picture of what strangles can do to a horse. But, where does it come from and what can you do about it?

The classic symptoms of a strangles infection include high fever, loss of appetite, thick discharge of pus from the nostrils and swelling in the lymph nodes located under the jaw. The swelling can become so great that it interferes with the horse's ability to breathe, which is where the name "strangles" originated.

Symptoms appear a few days to a week after exposure to the organism. A cough may be present, but cough is not a dramatic early symptom (as it is in viral upper-respiratory infections). Copious nasal discharge is obviously pus, being a white-to-yellow color and very thick. This, too, is different from viral infections where the nasal discharge, at least to start, is typically clear (this may change after several days to a week of a virus infection, if bacterial infection sets in, as well).

Swelling of the lymph nodes is typical. The involved nodes sit between the bones of the lower jaw, about midway along their length under the head. In a normal mature horse, you can barely feel them. In younger horses, they may be normally palpable as two semisoft structures about the size and shape of a peanut or smaller. With strangles, the bacteria travels to these lymph nodes where the reactive immune tissue in these glands fights hard to keep them from getting any further.

The body's predominant reaction is to set up a thick wall of connective tissue (the abscess wall) to produce a physical barrier to the

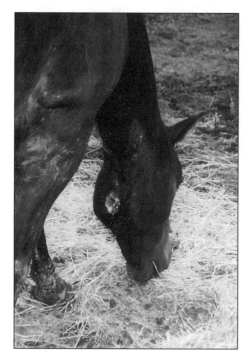

This horse shows a classic strangles lesion under the jaw. The organism will most likely contaminate his stall, waterer and bedding.

spread of the infection, while local white blood cells try to kill the bacteria. The lymph nodes and the abscesses they contain may swell to a great size.

Because of the anatomy of the area, this swelling will spread toward the back of the head/throat, where there is more room, and may sometimes extend back as far as the angle of the jaw, even up the sides of the jawbone.

For all the swelling you see on the outside of the head, swelling is equally occurring inside the throat as the lymph node abscesses grow. The sides of the horse's throat balloon inward and can cause a partial or near complete blockage to the flow of air. If severe enough, the horse may need an emergency tracheostomy (creation of a hole in the trachea — the "wind pipe").

Before the situation reaches this stage, however, the veterinarian will probably recommend that the abscesses be lanced (opened) to allow drainage to the outside. **Even with close veterinary care, the abscesses and associated edema may sometimes increase rapidly, causing an emergency situation with the horse unable to breathe.**

Strangles may also cause trouble with eating and swallowing. In any case, the horse will probably not feel much like doing either anyway — another reason close veterinary attention is important. A horse who is dehydrated and weakened will not fight his infection well. Intravenous fluids and nutrition may be needed to help support him in this critical stage.

Symptoms may last for weeks. Common sense can tell you when the horse is turning the corner. The nasal discharge will lessen and become less thick; lymph node size will decrease; fever will drop; and the horse will appear more alert, more willing to eat and drink.

How the horse gets infected

The *Streptococcus equi* bacteria are spread by direct contact —
horse to horse or infectious material (discharges containing the organism) to horse. The disease spreads quickly. Horses of any age
may be involved, but foals are most susceptible.

By adulthood, many horses have been exposed to strangles or have
been vaccinated, so they may not develop the disease as severely.
In fact, they may show no disease at all but still carry the bacteria
for a time. An adult horse who has not had prior exposure to strangles may become just as ill as a foal.

Although horses can pick up the infection from eating or drinking in areas contaminated with the strangles bacteria, the bacteria
does not survive for prolonged periods in the environment. **This
means that for strangles to get onto a farm, an infected horse usually must be involved.** In most situations, there is an index case (the
first-known case) who arrives at a farm after being infected, but before developing obvious symptoms. During this period he may min-
gle with other animals, potentially infecting them.

But, in some instances, there is no obvious index case, and the
animal responsible for the outbreak is difficult to identify. It may
be a horse who was exposed at a show or trail ride and carried the

*Strangles is passed from horse to horse. Horses new to a farm
should be isolated for two weeks before being turned out with
other horses or even being groomed with the same brushes.*

infection back with him, but had a strong enough immunity not to develop the disease himself. Another possibility is that one of the horses on the premises is a carrier.

A carrier is an animal who harbors an infectious organism and sheds it (releases it into the environment) without becoming ill. Horses who have recovered from strangles can shed the organism commonly for up to three months after the infection, some as long as 11 months. This is how some farms gain a reputation for having a "strangles problem." It is not the farm itself that is infected with strangles but one or more resident horses who have a prolonged carrier state, allowing new cases to develop year after year.

Once a horse has developed strangles, the horse must be isolated from other horses for at least three months and not worked or stressed during this time.

It is a widely held opinion that once a horse has had strangles he cannot develop the disease again. While this is true for most horses, a combination of circumstances, such as heavy stress at the time the horse is exposed to the organism, can override this natural protection.

The organism

Strangles is caused by the bacteria Streptococcus equi. There are many Streptococci (plural for Streptococcus) found throughout nature. Some are fairly harmless. Some are destructive, like strangles. Yet others are actually beneficial, like the Streptococci that live in the intestinal tract and help process food.

Under the microscope, Streptococci appear as tiny, round beads. They stain deeply with a special stain called a Gram stain, and this puts them into the category of the Gram-positive bacteria. Gram-positive bacteria are known to be sensitive to specific types of antibiotics, notably the penicillin family and other drugs that work on the metabolism of the bacteria in similar ways.

Streptococcus equi is considered to be a highly species-specific bacterium, meaning that disease from this organism is limited to horses. While this is true in most cases, the bacteria have also been isolated from related species (camels and burros), where they were not causing any disease but were quietly living in the upper-respiratory tract tissues of these animals. This means there is a potential for similar species to carry the Streptococcus equi bacteria to horses without becoming ill themselves.

You should also know there is a reported case of severe illness in a human caused by Streptococcus equi. This is an extremely unusual situation, however, and would not occur under most natural conditions, unless the person received a large dose of bacteria through an area of broken skin or had another active disease condition at the time that would compromise normal immune responses.

The strangles bacteria gain access to the horse's body in much the same way a cold or flu virus does — through the lining of the upper-respiratory tract in the nose and throat. *In most cases, the horse's immune system immediately reacts and keeps the organism from progressing any further. However, with massive infections and/or immature or compromised immune status, the bacteria can spread and cause problems in a variety of other locations.*

"Bastard" strangles

"Bastard" strangles is the spread of the organism to other parts of the horse's body, such as the guttural pouches, the air-filled sacs located along the sides of the throat, just behind the angle of the jaw. They open into the upper throat through two slit-like openings that are visible with an endoscope. Because these pouches are close to the infected tissues, they are at high risk for being involved with strangles. If infection gains access to this area, swelling will occur along the back edge of the jaw bone, giving the horse's head a blown-up appearance. The guttural pouches can fill with a thick pus that does not drain easily.

Because there are important arterial and nervous structures lying close to the guttural pouches, treatment of this complication is critical. The veterinarian will most likely use an endoscope and pass catheters/tubes inside the guttural pouches to flush them out and instill medications. These tubes may be left in place to provide an avenue of drainage for the pus and allow further treatments.

The strangles bacteria have the potential to spread to virtually anywhere in the horse's body. **With a horse who is not fighting the infection well and has extensive body-wide involvement, the chance of death from complications is high.** In many other cases, however-er, it may only be a small number of organisms that escape the local immune reaction to find a resting place elsewhere in the body.

This small focus of infection may be completely unsuspected by you or the veterinarian. The horse may either successfully kill these bacteria or may only be able to slow down their multiplication by forming an abscess inside his body. The horse may then carry this abscess for the rest of his life.

SYMPTOMS APPEAR A FEW DAYS TO A WEEK

AFTER EXPOSURE TO THE ORGANISM.

A COUGH MAY BE PRESENT BUT IS NOT A

DRAMATIC EARLY SYMPTOM.

Some such abscesses cause no real problems for the horse. Other horses may be symptom-free until the abscess reaches a large size. This typically occurs in the abdomen, where an abscess may grow unsuspected or undiagnosed for years until it becomes large enough to interfere with intestinal function.

If the abscess forms in an area that is subjected to a lot of move-ment, for example, inside the chest, the horse may show a long his-tory of having problems with a lack of appetite, not performing well or having low-grade fevers for no obvious reason.

What may be happening is that the abscess is periodically moved and pulled enough to cause small breaks in the abscess wall that leak bacteria. This makes the horse a little sick until the abscess again becomes sealed off. This can go on for a long time until the abscess becomes big enough to cause a serious problem or develops a large enough leak to make the horse really sick.

If large numbers of bacteria/large amounts of toxin gain access to the horse's blood stream, complications involving abnormalities of blood clotting can result. The horse may develop hemorrhages throughout the body and on the mucus membranes of the mouth.

Edema of the legs and abdomen, possibly with oozing of fluids through the skin, can occur. This is a life-threatening complication. **Any horse with strangles who begins to show fluid build-up should be immediately seen by a veterinarian and will probably require intensive care in a veterinary hospital.**

Treatment of strangles

Although the strangles bacteria are sensitive to antibiotics, veterinarians debate about using them. Arguments against antibiotic use in every case is that the antibiotic may slow the development and maturation of the local abscesses. There is also concern that some bacteria may escape the antibiotics (because thick-walled abscesses can keep them out), and the antibiotics may actually end up slowing the resolution of disease. Some vets also prefer to let the strangles run its course, in hopes the horse will have a stronger immunity after he recovers.

On the opposite side of this argument are those who feel that because of the potential life-threatening complications of strangles, all horses should be treated with antibiotics.

Most veterinarians steer a middle course. Cases that are relatively mild and show good development of abscesses will be watched closely without giving antibiotics. Horses who have high fevers and are not coping well with the infection will be treated with antibiotics. Any horse showing signs of complications should receive antibiotics.

The veterinarian will usually take cultures from several horses involved in an outbreak and send those to a lab for culture and sensitivity testing. The culture confirms which specific bacterium is involved, and the sensitivity test indicates which antibiotics the bacteria are sensitive to.

Strangles bacteria are historically sensitive to penicillin and the penicillin family of antibiotics. Most horses will be treated first with penicillin, switching to or adding other antibiotics if response to treatment is poor. The veterinarian may decide to use higher doses than normal of this antibiotic in hopes of achieving better blood levels inside abscesses. Penicillin may be given intravenously initially, then switched to intramuscularly. Samples for culture and sensitivity are taken again if the infection does not respond well.

General supportive measures include intravenous fluid/intravenous feeding, judicious use of anti-inflammatory drugs such as phenylbutazone to combat high fevers, and hot packs applied to abscesses to encourage them to come to a head and break. Once an abscessed area has broken open, it will need to be flushed out one or more times a day and the skin around the area cleaned, then protected with petroleum jelly.

What to do in a strangles outbreak

Once strangles is documented, or even strongly suspected, immediately divide the horses into three groups. **Group I** *is the sick horses.* **Group II** *is all horses that are not yet sick but have had direct contact with the ones that are sick.* **Group III** *is horses that have not had direct contact with sick horses but are on the same premises.*

Group I *horses must be strictly isolated and treated, but should not be vaccinated. They should not be returned to the herd, or share any turnout facilities or equipment, for at least three months after all signs of illness are gone and any abscessed areas have healed. These horses may pose a threat to other animals even after they seem to have recovered. Do at least three throat cultures before deciding the horse is safe to return to contact with other horses.*

Group II *horses should have their temperatures taken and be carefully examined twice a day for any signs of nasal discharge or lymph-node swelling. At the first signs of fever or symptoms, these horses should be moved to Group I. If no symptoms develop after seven days, the horses may be vaccinated and moved in with the Group III horses.*

Wash your hands with hot water and an over-the-counter antibacterial soap, such as Dial, after handling one horse and before handling another.

Group III *horses should be vaccinated when strangles is* *present on a farm. It may not prevent the disease, but it may decrease the severity of disease, should they contract it.*

Most new cases can be expected to appear within seven days of the first case. However, you cannot let your guard down after seven days. Take the temperature of every horse at least once a day and watch carefully for other symptoms. Horses never vaccinated for strangles before will take about 10 days to two weeks to develop a good level of antibodies. Even after this time, protection is still not 100 percent.

You can — and should — disinfect stalls, buckets, grooming supplies and equipment that may have been contaminated by the secretions of infected horses, but you can't completely eradicate all traces of the bacteria from the barn and/or turnout facilities. As new cases develop, even if they had been vaccinated, they must be moved to Group I.

Vaccination for strangles

Because bacteria are more complex organisms than viruses, it is far more difficult to develop an effective vaccine for bacteria than for viruses. Researchers have been able to identify specific proteins in the *Streptococcus equi* bacterium that induce an immune response, and these are used in vaccines.

Unfortunately, reactions to the injectable vaccine are common. Many horses develop a swelling, often large, at the site of the vaccination. If there was any laxity in using strict sterile techniques before vaccinating, these swellings turn into abscesses.

Another problem with strangles vaccines is that the immunity they induce is not strong. **The vaccine may reduce the severity of the disease but not necessarily completely protect the horse from infection.**

Strangles vaccination is not routinely administered. Exceptions to this include farms where strangles has been a recurrent problem — usually breeding farms — and for individual horses who must enter such a farm. The usual program is to vaccinate mares two to four weeks before they foal. This is done for protection of the mare, but also to make sure her milk will contain antibodies against strangles to help protect the foal. Horses who are not in this high-risk group are usually not vaccinated.

For strangles intranasal vaccination, the vaccine is sprayed into the horse's nose, through a thin tube attached to a syringe.

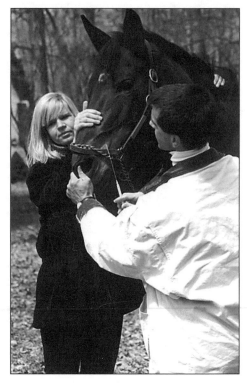

If your horse is not being bred, the decision of whether or not to vaccinate must depend on how high a risk there is of infection. Factors to consider include the amount of traffic on and off the farm where the horse is located, whether or not there is a recent (less than a year) history of strangles on the farm and whether the horse travels off the farm and is in contact with many other horses. Your veterinarian can best guide you on reaching this decision.

The most recent development in strangles vaccines is an intranasal vaccine — spraying the vaccine into the nasal passages. So far it is at least as effective as the intramuscular injection and has none of the problematic local side effects. **The intranasal vaccine results in the production of antibodies in the tissues of the horse's upper respiratory tract that greatly boost the first line of defense against this infection.**

Other prevention measures

Preventing strangles boils down to minimizing the horse's chance of exposure. Much of this is common sense and involves measures you would take to protect for any infectious disease.

■ When away from home, do not allow the horse to graze or eat/drink from any buckets that are not yours.

■ Do not put a horse into a strange stall when away from home unless you check into the history of recent infectious disease on the premises first and/or know the stall was disinfected before your arrival. (This may mean you disinfect a stall before stabling at a show.)

■ At home, new horses should be strictly isolated for one week to 10 days. Do not put the new horse into any stall or turnout facilities used by other horses. When possible, get a detailed history on the newcomer, as well as any exposure to illnesses he may have had.

■ If a new horse is showing some vague symptoms or came from a farm with strangles, consider having your veterinarian do one or more cultures of the horse's throat. ▣

Notes

18

A Thyroid Problem?

Does every older, shaggy horse or middle-aged, lethargic, obese horse have a thyroid problem? We'll unravel the truths and myths.

W hen most people hear "thyroid problem," they think of obesity. **However, the thyroid gland does a lot more than influence weight by controlling how rapidly the body burns calories.** And, while problems related to thyroid gland function — both hypothyroidism (too low) and hyperthyroidism (too high) — can have a major impact on the horse's entire body, they occur less frequently in horses than in humans or dogs, most people's frame of reference for this health problem.

Every horse has an individual metabolic rate — the speed at which he uses fuel and what he stores as fat — regulated by his thyroid. However, most fall within a similar range, with a few variances according to breed. Horses bred for speed, such as Thoroughbreds, tend to have higher metabolic rates than horses bred for slower work, like draft breeds, or horses who survive well under harsh conditions (most pony breeds). A higher metabolic rate is reflected in how much feed per pound of body weight it takes to keep body weight stable; "racey" and high-strung types need more feed than more even-tempered horses or ponies.

Thyroid status often also influences body temperature. Low thyroid status and slow metabolic rates result in lower body temperatures, while high levels of thyroid hormone and high metabolic rates correspond to higher body temperatures. **In fact, in people and animals, one of the earliest signs of an underactive thyroid is intolerance to cold, while those who are hyperthyroid always feel**

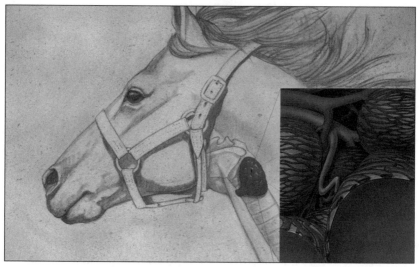

ILLUSTRATION: KIP CARTER

The thyroid gland is located in the upper portion of the neck, usually on the left side. It rests up against the trachea (windpipe). In normal horses, the thyroid may be difficult to feel. In horses with an enlarged thyroid (goiter), it is easy to feel and may even be visible as a swelling or lump in this area

too warm. At least part of the explanation for this phenomenon is that high metabolic rates and rapid burning of calories produces more heat, and vice versa.

The thyroid gland is also important in maintaining normal growth in young animals. **When thyroid function is low, growth suffers. The rate of cell division slows, and stunting can result.** Multiple factors also may be at work, such as problems with other hormones or malnutrition. However, uncomplicated hypothyroidism can have this effect on its own.

The thyroid has many effects on muscle, including an influence on how much blood supply it receives, how sensitive it is to impulses initiating contraction and how quickly it recovers the ability to contract. Abnormalities of thyroid function (both hypo- and hyperthyroidism) have a profound impact on muscle strength and exercise tolerance. Thyroid-hormone levels also influence how well muscles use their major source of energy, carbohydrates. **The influence of thyroid hormone on muscle is important in understanding some of the common symptoms seen in horses with low thyroid-hormone levels.**

Finally, thyroid status can influence reproductive performance. Horses with low thyroid function have lower libido (sex drive) and lower fertility.

Symptoms of hypothyroidism

Cresty necks, lazy attitudes, obesity and laminitis/founder have been blamed on low-thyroid problems. However, the facts are not clear. On one hand, horses who are overweight and lazy may show improvement when given thyroid-hormone supplements. But, on the other hand, blood tests of thyroid-hormone levels in those same horses often show values that are within normal ranges. It is not surprising that supplementing thyroid hormone has a beneficial effect in overweight and lazy horses. The question, however, is whether this is because they are deficient to start with or simply because the horses are actually being overdosed and showing a reaction that is more related to hyperthyroidism in their specific cases.

HYPERTHYROIDISM SHOWS UP IN HORSES ONLY WHEN THEY ARE OVERSUPPLEMENTED WITH IODINE OR THYROID HORMONES.

Popular horseowner opinion often links laminitis and hypothyroidism, but there is no solid proof that true hypothyroidism is involved in founder. Horses and ponies who are overweight and cresty-necked are prone to founder, but the cause of their founder is not usually a thyroid problem.

Diseases of the thyroid gland rarely cause hypothyroidism in horses. However, a syndrome of decreased thyroid-hormone level is sometimes seen in horses who are under a great deal of stress, whether from heavy work, serious diseases or injuries. Muscle soreness, decreased exercise tolerance and tying-up are common complaints that sometimes can be traced to hypothyroidism in working horses.

While you might expect horses with hypothyroidism to be overweight, sometimes hypothyroid horses are underweight because they may have poor appetites. An exception to this is horses who

Older horses who show a loss of muscle tissue or who fail to shed their winter coats should be checked for hormone problems.

have low thyroid-hormone levels associated with other abnormalities, such as pituitary tumors.

Nonspecific symptoms may include a low heart rate, low to low-normal body temperature, dull attitude, poor performance, low-grade anemia and a dull haircoat.

Diagnosis of thyroid problems

If a thyroid problem is suspected, the veterinarian will do a physical examination to see if the thyroid gland feels normal (see goiter below). If the veterinarian is familiar with the horse's vital signs (temperature, pulse and respiration) from examination in the past, changes may be noted. A history of appetite, weight or attitude changes and muscle problems is suggestive, although none of these things can confirm the diagnosis.

Only blood tests can confirm a thyroid problem. Many chemistry screens look at T4, the inactive form of thyroid hormone, and most veterinarians see low T4 as indicating hypothyroidism. However, there is some debate about whether this is enough to make the diagnosis. Some also test for T3 (the active form) and TSH (the thyroid-stimulating hormone), as there are some conditions in other species where T4 could be low but T3 and TSH normal or even high.

This debate remains unsettled, and for now most veterinarians rely on T4 for the diagnosis.

Symptoms of hyperthyroidism

Hyperthyroidism caused by a disease state in the thyroid or other controlling glands is essentially nonexistent in horses. However, hyperthyroidism caused by oversupplementation with iodine or thyroid-hormone replacements occurs with some regularity, so you should know the symptoms:

- *Anxious attitude.*
- *Easy sweating.*
- *Weight loss.*
- *Either a voracious or depressed appetite.*
- *Muscle problems such as pain, cramping or tying-up.*

Possible nonspecific symptoms include high heart rate and high-normal to slightly high temperature. Veterinarians often describe this as the horse "burning himself up." It is easy to induce hyperthyroidism inadvertently by oversupplementation, so if your veterinarian prescribes thyroid supplements, carefully follow all recommendations for periodic blood tests to check on the hormone levels, and never give more than the recommended dose.

Disorders affecting thyroid function

■ **Goiter: Goiter is an enlargement of the thyroid gland.** It can occur when there is either too much iodine (resulting in hyperthyroidism) or too little (causing hypothyroidism) in the diet. Most diets are low in iodine, but many supplements or fortified grain mixes add this trace mineral. Thyroid hormones contain iodine. Without enough iodine, the level of hormone will fall. With too much, the thyroid gland is overstimulated.

Goiter has occurred in mares and foals eating iodine-deficient diets. It has also been caused by overuse of high-iodine supplements, such as kelp. If your horse develops a swelling in the area of the thyroid, check with your veterinarian or a nutritionist about the possibility of an iodine-related goiter. (Note: The iodized salt you find on the grocery shelf was designed to prevent goiter caused by low iodine in humans.)

■ **Pituitary tumors:** TSH, a hormone released by the pituitary gland in the brain, controls how much thyroid hormone is produced.

   One of the more common tumors in older horses and ponies involves the pituitary gland. This tumor can cause production of TSH to slow down or cease, resulting in hypothyroidism.

   This is only one part of the hormonal problems caused by pituitary tumors. In addition to the hypothyroidism, other classic symptoms are a long hair coat, failure to shed out, a pot-bellied appearance (this comes from muscle weakness), loss of muscle mass and excessive water intake with high urine output.

■ **Role of stress:** It is not clear how stress plays a role in thyroid function. But a simplified explanation is that the body senses it is under attack (from heavy exercise demands, illness, severe wound, etc.) and reacts by trying to conserve all energy for vital functions, such as keeping the brain intact and the heart working smoothly.

   Part of this complicated defense mechanism is to slow the production of thyroid hormone. **By diverting energy and blood supply away from the muscles and (in the case of growing animals) growing tissues, the brain and circulatory system receive maximal supplies.**

Thyroid products should only be used when a thyroid problem has been diagnosed and the proper thyroid supplement and dosage prescribed by your veterinarian.

Production of other hormones, such as the stress hormones ("adrenalin"/epinephrine), may also be suppressed when the horse is under a lot of stress.

■ **Role of diet:** We have already mentioned how iodine levels can affect thyroid function. Other factors proven to affect the thyroid (at least in other species) include calorie intake and quality of the protein in the diet. **Basically, horses who do not get enough carbohydrate calories and those who receive low levels of poor-quality protein may develop hypothyroidism.**

Treatment of thyroid problems

Hyperthyroidism shows up in horses *only* when they are over-supplemented with iodine or thyroid hormones. The solution is simple — stop giving these things.

With hypothyroidism, the first step is to look for and eliminate underlying causes, such as nutritional factors and stress. Hypothyroidism is often temporary and goes away when the underlying problems are corrected. In the meantime, the horse can be supplemented with either iodine, if that is the problem, or thyroid-replacement products, per your veterinarian's instructions.

Thyroid replacement products are of two types — those that include active thyroid hormone and those that are extracts of thyroid glands. The latter have some thyroid hormone activity, but not as much as hormone preparations, and also contain iodine and possibly unidentified factors that help promote a healthy thyroid. Your veterinarian should choose the products for treatment. Remember, too, that regular monitoring of blood thyroid-hormone levels is extremely important. As the thyroid gland begins to function normally again, you will reduce the dose of the replacement products gradually, eventually stopping them.

Thyroid function in the older horse

Older horses are more likely than younger horses to develop tumors of the pituitary gland, the "master gland." This gland is located within the brain and is responsible for controlling the function of every other gland in the body. When a tumor develops, the effects will depend on which portion of the pituitary is involved. In most cases, pituitary tumors result in more than one gland showing abnormal function. Compared to other problems caused by pituitary tumors, hypothyroidism is relatively easy to remedy, improving the quality of the horse's life.

Older horses are also more likely to have outside forces affect thyroid function. These would include chronic stress (less able to compete in a group, chronic illnesses such as arthritis) and nutritional inadequacies caused by other horses getting more of a share of the feed, bad teeth with inefficient chewing and decreased efficiency of digestion.

Any older horse showing symptoms of decreased energy, loss of appetite, loss of muscle tissue, poor hair coat and hoof quality, and weight loss should at least be checked for thyroid-hormone function. We are not suggesting that all such problems are due to low thyroid function, as any of these can be seen quite commonly in older horses and can have many different causes. However, hypothyroidism can contribute both to their development and their worsening.

Treatment for such horses involves providing a highly digestible diet with high-quality protein and supplemental minerals (including iodine in the appropriate amounts). The veterinarian will decide if supplemental thyroid hormone is also indicated. ▣

19

Tying Up Unraveled

Tying up happens at the cellular level.
Understanding how muscles function
is the key to sorting out folklore from science.

Tying up is a condition in the horse characterized by muscle cramping, obvious pain, brown discoloration of the urine and reluctance to move. **Triggered by exercise or excitement, tying up is really a symptom, not a specific disease.** It happens when a horse's muscles have been greatly overworked and damaged by toxic by-products produced during that work. However, tying up can have many different causes — which is why one horse may respond well to a certain treatment while another horse does not respond at all.

Tying up is an indicator that something is wrong in the exercise sequence of energy-generation, work and recovery. A horse who is tying up becomes progressively slower and resistant to continuing work, until either you stop working him because something is obviously wrong or the horse simply freezes in his tracks. Nonspecific signs of pain — sweating, rapid breathing with flaring of the nostrils and rapid pulse rate — are all present. The temperature may be elevated or normal.

The horse will stand very rigidly, as if bracing himself, and will resist any attempts to move him. The large muscle groups of the hind end will feel very hard to the touch, and the horse may exhibit pain when you touch them. Shifting of weight from one foot to the other, while only lifting them slightly, is sometimes seen. The penis may be dropped in geldings and stallions, and/or they may drip urine.

189

A horse who is tying up may stand stiffly or be reluctant to move, as if his hindquarters were frozen.

However, many horses are unwilling or unable to assume the position to urinate and/or exert abdominal pressure because of pain from the sore muscles. In moderate to severe cases of tying up, the urine is discolored — from a reddish brown to brown to brownish black color. When the horse urinates for the first time after tying up, the urine stream may initially be yellow, changing to dark.

A medical emergency

If you think your horse is tying up, call the vet immediately. Do not attempt to walk a horse that has tied up; even slow, low-level exercise can worsen the muscle damage. Bring a trailer to the horse to ship him back to the barn. Protect the horse from chills with a light blanket, especially across the hindquarters, which do most of the horse's muscular work and are therefore the worst affected. If you are away from the barn, use your jacket to cover his hindquarters. Remove the saddle or at least loosen the girth to make the horse more comfortable.

While waiting for the vet, hose the horse (weather permitting) with warm water over his entire body for 10 to 15 minutes. This helps the muscles to relax and helps restore body temperature to normal. Scrape the water off and cover him with a light sheet.

Encourage the horse to drink to help flush his kidneys and hasten the clearance of waste material. Have a bucket of fresh water and a bucket of electrolyte water within the horse's easy reach. To make electrolyte water, use any powdered electrolyte or electrolyte/dextrose mix for horses or any other farm animal (dairy cow, calf, etc.). The horse, however, may not be willing to drink. It is common for the vet to give the horse fluids intravenously or by stomach tube.

Bed the stall very heavily to provide a deep cushion in case the horse feels he must lie down.

To understand tying up and why it can be so difficult to figure out and treat correctly, you need to understand the steps involved in muscular activity. The problem occurs at one or more of these steps in the muscle contraction and relaxation processes.

The contraction process

■ **Electrolyte shifts:** Movement of sodium and potassium across the muscle cell (potassium out of the cell, sodium in) is critical in initiating muscle contraction and in controlling the degree of contraction. (It is also critical in allowing the muscle to relax.)

■ **Energy generation:** Microscopic bonds within a muscle keep it lined up along its resting length. Contraction requires energy to break these bonds. The muscle gets this energy from two high-energy sources: creatine phosphate and ATP. A certain amount of creatine phosphate and ATP are stored within the muscle itself. These stores are immediately available for energy release, which means that the muscle cell does not need any outside help to use them — no blood supply, oxygen or food. These power sources are used up very quickly, however. To continue working, the muscle burns fuel to replace the ATP as quickly as it is being used up. (Creatine phosphate stores are not replaced until after work is stopped.) The fuels used depend upon the level of exercise.

During hard/fast work, such as racing or pulling a heavy load, most fuel replacement is performed without the benefit of oxygen and is called "anaerobic" ("an" = without, "aerobic" = oxygen). This happens because the blood cannot supply enough oxygen to keep up with the demand and because the energy pathways that use oxygen simply take too long to keep up with the energy need. The only fuel suitable for anaerobic energy generation is carbohydrate. Horses' muscle cells contain a generous store of carbohydrate called "glycogen."

"Aerobic" work, which is less intense than a flat-out effort, burns fuel using available oxygen from the blood supply. Exactly how much work an individual horse can perform aerobically depends on his level of conditioning. Unfit horses can do much less aerobic work than horses in consistent training. Fuels used for aerobic work include glycogen from the muscles, glucose from the blood and fats from the blood. (Protein and ketones are two other energy fuels that can be used, but their contribution is very small under normal circumstances.)

Two minerals, calcium and magnesium, are critically involved as well in the contraction process.

Factors affecting tying up

Sex: Some studies show slightly more fillies and mares have tying up problems than males; others do not confirm this. Some feel the typical candidate for tying up is a nervous filly. If this is a valid observation, it could be that low-level muscle pain, present prior to a full-blown problem, causes nervous behavior, rather than tying up being the result of gender or nervousness.

Weather: While horses can and do tie up year round, some people think cold weather causes tying up. If cold weather is a trigger in some horses, the reason is not immediately obvious. Inadequate warm-up prior to work may play a role.

Prior history: A horse who has tied up in the past does have a higher risk of doing so in the future.

Confinement: Unexpected stall confinement may precipitate tying up, especially in a horse who is very fit and is kept on full grain feeding. The exact mechanism for this is not yet known, but it appears to be related to changes in metabolism that are induced by training, allowing the horse to produce large amounts of energy. In horses deprived of their regular exercise, something goes wrong, and their muscle overreacts on the next bout of exercise.

The relaxation process

To relax, a muscle breaks down connections that are created during contraction between the tiny muscle cells, allowing the muscle to return to its resting-state length. This process also requires energy generated in the same way as the energy for contraction. Calcium and magnesium again are involved, as is reversal of the direction of the flow of potassium and sodium across the cell.

In the process of generating all this energy for contraction and relaxation, the burning of fuels creates some nasty by-products that can damage the cells. There is also a considerable amount of heat created and an increase in muscle cell acidity (the pH). The body normally controls and reverses these potentially harmful conditions that arise both during exercise and in the recovery phase.

THE GOAL OF SUPPLEMENTATION IS TO
KEEP ALL KEY ELECTROLYTE LEVELS IN
THE HIGH-TO-NORMAL RANGE.

Things that go wrong

This description of how muscle works indicates how complicated this process is. There are many more details to the process, but you now have enough of a background to understand where the problems arise and how they can be corrected.

■ **Electrolyte shifts:** Problems resulting in tying up can occur as two different types — the amount of sodium and potassium inside and outside the cell or a change in the "sodium potassium pumps," the structures within the cell that move sodium and potassium in and out.

A low potassium level inside the cell is the most likely imbalance problem to occur. This can contribute to tying up by causing cramping. However, severe tying up, with dark urine, is not likely to occur from low potassium alone.

Do not attempt to move a horse who is tying up. Cover his hindquarters with a sheet or your jacket if necessary, and stay with him until help arrives.

Changes in the number of sodium potassium pumps on the cell surface can cause tying up. Abnormally low numbers make the cell weaker and more easily overworked than normal. Higher numbers of pumps make the muscle more sensitive, more likely to "over-react" to the nerve impulses to contract, performing more work than needed. Abnormal thyroid hormone levels are the most common cause of these problems. High thyroid levels cause higher numbers of sodium potassium pumps and vice versa.

■ **The contraction process:** The steps involved in generating energy for muscular work are at the root of the most common cause of tying up: overwork. Overwork does not necessarily mean that you take the horse out and deliberately work him too hard (although this will do it, too!). It simply means that he was worked beyond the level his muscles are conditioned to perform comfortably.

A horse working beyond his level of conditioning must perform much of the work anaerobically. This causes more rapid drops in muscle pH (an increase in acidity) and generates considerable heat, making the muscle work inefficiently. The waste products produced (called "free radicals") are toxic and damage the cells. Energy stores begin to run low, and damaged cells may leak critical electrolytes. The result is more damaged cells, with cramping and local swelling.

■ **The relaxation process:** The same things that interfere with efficient contraction (i.e., calcium, magnesium or potassium losses, build-up of damaging waste products and low energy stores) also prevent the muscle from relaxing completely. This gives the horse the typical "tied-up" appearance.

Attacking the problem

There is rarely one single problem that causes any particular horse to tie up. Instead, investigation will usually uncover more than one abnormality that must be corrected for optimal treatment.

The place to begin is with a complete blood chemistry screen. Of special importance are the levels of blood calcium, blood magnesium, blood potassium, blood T4 (thyroid hormone) and the enzymes CPK and SGOT.

The first three tests tell the veterinarian the degree to which the major electrolytes are out of balance. Electrolyte imbalances are treated by giving supplemental electrolytes, either orally or (initially) intravenously. The test results help design treatment for the acute problem as well as a maintenance program to help the muscles function at their best.

The thyroid hormone level is extremely important, as either very high or very low levels can cause tying up. Elevated thyroid hormone levels (hyperthyroidism) rarely, if ever, occur naturally. They can result from an oversupply of either supplemental thyroid hormone or an organic source of iodine. Removal of the excess is the treatment.

Hypothyroidism, or low levels, is more common but is sometimes difficult to pinpoint accurately with available tests. T4 is generally the most reliable indicator of thyroid function. The veterinarian will usually place a tying-up horse with an obviously low T4 level on thyroid replacement therapy.

The muscle enzyme levels (CPK, SGOT) tell the veterinarian how badly the muscles are damaged. These enzymes leak out of damaged cells, and the higher the level, the worse the damage. This information is important in deciding how long to rest the horse and in making recommendations for the resumption of exercise. **Also, monitoring these enzyme levels enables the veterinarian to tell when the horse is on the road to recovery and whether or not the chosen therapy is working.**

In treating the acute problem, the veterinarian will also often use intravenous fluids (to prevent damage to the kidneys by the circulating muscle pigment, myoglobin), muscle relaxant drugs (such as ace-promazine and robaxin) and sodium bicarbonate to correct over-acidity, if present.

The nutritional aspect of treatment

The goal of supplementation is to keep all key electrolyte levels in the high-normal range. Particular emphasis must be placed on potassium, calcium and magnesium, and blood levels should be monitored to assure adequate intake.

Potassium must be supplemented until the problem is under control, since even mild episodes of tying up can result in significant potassium loss from the muscle cells. Calcium and magnesium supplementation guidelines depend on the diet, especially the type of hay being used. Legume hays (alfalfa) are very rich in calcium and also contain good levels of magnesium. However, many horses on alfalfa are found to have low blood magnesium levels. The mechanism for this is uncertain but may have something to do with the large amount of calcium competing with the magnesium for absorption.

Damage from toxic waste products can be arrested and prevented in the future by the use of correct amounts of substances termed "antioxidants," which prevent free radical damage to the cells. Free radicals are highly reactive, electrically charged molecules produced during exercise. The major antioxidants are actually very familiar substances — vitamin E, vitamin C and selenium. **Supplementation will go a long way in preventing tying up.** This is especially true in areas of the United States (along both coasts, Great Lakes region) that have low levels of selenium in the soil, leading to deficiencies.

Many combination vitamin E/selenium products are on the market, and you will need veterinary advice to match one to your local soil and feed/hay selenium levels. Initial selenium supplementation should probably be in the form of injection, since for reasons that are not well understood, absorption of selenium in the oral form can be unpredictable. Better absorption is obtained by using a chelated form of selenium.

High levels of vitamin C (7 to 20 grams per day) and vitamin E (10,000 I.U. per day) are beneficial in the early treatment stages of tying up and until muscle enzyme levels have returned to normal. After this, maintenance on vitamin C at a minimum of 4.5 grams per day and vitamin E at 5,000 to 8,000 I.U. per day is helpful in preventing muscle damage in working horses. You can also give the

The muscles on the horse's back and hindquarters will feel very hard and, when touched, may be painful to the horse.

horse the benefit of the powerful natural antioxidant, lipoic acid, by feeding extra virgin olive oil, which contains extremely high levels of this nutrient.

Supplemental B vitamins are sometimes recommended for treatment of tying up. **Many of the B vitamins play a key role in the normal metabolism of carbohydrate — the main fuel for muscle.** Of special importance is thiamine. Deficiencies of thiamine classically cause cramping and elevated blood lactate and pyruvate levels — findings typical of tying up. Thiamine supplementation at a rate of 500 to 1,000 mg is often very effective and should be combined with a good multiple B supplement.

Monday-morning sickness

In the days of work horses plowing the field, tying up often happened on Monday morning. This is because the horses worked hard all week, and on the weekend they received the same feed rations, even though they weren't exerting themselves. The usual scenario was that the team started plowing and then froze in their tracks. Tying

> *up has also been referred to as "corded up," "seized up"*
> *or "set fast." The technical name for tying up is "azoturia"*
> *or "exertional myopathy."*
>
> *Not all horses who tie up fall into the Monday-morning*
> *picture. Horses can tie up as a result of any exertion or*
> *excitement, and it can be a one-time occurrence or hap-*
> *pen a number of times. Tying up has been reported in*
> *veterinary textbooks for over 100 years.*

The role of grain and protein

Recovery from tying up also requires a high-quality diet with an appropriate level of high-quality protein, such as soybean or alfalfa meal or milk protein. (Calf Manna is a good protein supplement to use.) Feeding grain to horses who have tied up is often a point of hot contention. Grain is the horse's major source of readily absorbable carbohydrate — the muscle fuel. Although it is a widely held opinion that feeding grain causes tying up, exactly what happens is far from perfectly clear. Recent research shows that tying up involves some defect in the processing of carbohydrate by the muscle. Whether this is a basic defect in horses who tie up, a change related to heavy training or perhaps a nutritional deficiency that can be corrected by proper supplementation remains to be seen.

It does appear that high grain feeding combined with restriction of exercise (stall confinement), especially in horses accustomed to regular, heavy work, can precipitate tying up. It is advisable to cut grain rations drastically on any day when stall confinement is unavoidable. Make every effort to provide some form of exercise every day to horses who have a tendency to tie up, even if it is only walking up and down the barn aisle for 20 to 30 minutes.

Increasing fat in the diet may also help some horses who tie up. Fat is a very efficient alternative energy source for horses, especially if their work is primarily aerobic (low-to-moderate intensity). **Feeding fat causes the enzyme systems within the muscle cell that burn fat to increase their activity.** This helps to conserve the important carbohydrate energy stores. You can either switch to one of the new high-fat feeds or add fat in the form of corn oil (together with the olive oil). Consult your veterinarian for guidelines on introducing fat. As a general rule, corn oil is tolerated well and is beneficial up to a level of two cups per day.

The truth about lactate

No discussion of tying up would be complete without mention of lactate/lactic acid. Just about everyone has heard that lactic acid causes tying up, and there are many products on the market that claim to treat or prevent tying up by eliminating lactic acid.

*Let's begin by making one thing clear: **Lactic acid does not cause tying up.***

*Lactic acid is a normal end product of anaerobic energy generation from carbohydrates. In high-intensity work loads, lactate production is extremely high, since the amount of work being done requires rapid energy production that cannot be achieved in any other way. The harder the horse works, the more lactate is produced. A horse who has just won a race will have extremely high lactates — as will a horse who has just finished pulling a very heavy load. The fact that lactate is high after high intensity work has led some people to assume the lactate accumulation is what causes fatigue or even muscle damage. However, research has shown that this is not the case. **If all other conditions for continued work are being met (i.e., adequate electrolyte levels and adequate blood flow), it is the depletion of carbohydrate energy stores that causes fatigue.** If more carbohydrates were available, the horse would keep right on going and produce even more lactate!*

High-intensity work is always associated with high lactic-acid levels. However, lower work loads that can be done under aerobic conditions result in less lactate accumulation. As a horse is trained under aerobic work loads, he becomes more and more efficient at using the lactate produced as a fuel for continued work, resulting in lower and lower lactic-acid levels after work as the horse becomes fit.

When a horse has tied up, lactate levels are often very high. This may be because he was overworked, because of a nutritional insufficiency (i.e., thiamine) or because of some alteration still not understood in how carbohydrate is metabolized. In this situation, the high lactates are a marker that something has gone wrong, but they are not the cause of the problem.

Other therapies

Talk with your veterinarian about two products that may help your particular horse.

Dantrolene is a relative of the antiseizure drug Dilantin. It has a very specific action on muscle cells, slowing down the release of stored intracellular calcium, which also slows contraction. It is most helpful for horses who have a particularly severe form of tying up termed "malignant hyperthermia." This disease is relatively rare compared to other causes of tying up but should be suspected if episodes are very frequent, if there is a history of tying up in the horse's family or if the horse always has abnormally high muscle-enzyme levels.

RVI is a fairly new product with a different approach to the problem of tying up. RVI is actually an inactivated virus that works by influencing the immune system. The muscle damage in tying up causes the body to mount an inflammatory reaction. The inflammatory reaction involves release of enzymes from white blood cells whose job is to "clean up," but that can actually make matters worse. It is believed RVI works at this level. While this drug can be very effective, it is not a cure and should only be used in combination with efforts to correct any imbalances and to get to the cause of the problem. ▣

Reference Information

Normal Physiological Data for Adult Horses

Temperature: 99° to 101° F
Pulse: High 20s to low 40s beats per minute
Respiration: 8 to 20 breaths per minute
Mucous membrane color: Pale pink to medium pink
Capillary refill time: 1 to 3 seconds
Note: All figures will be higher for foals. Weather conditions and time of day will cause variances in these numbers.

Parts of the Horse

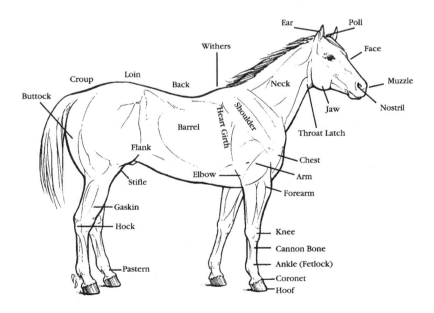

Information for Emergencies

Emergencies requiring an immediate call to the veterinarian:

- Abdominal pain (sweating, rolling, kicking at belly, looking at belly, lying down, blowing hard)

- Eye injury

- Refusal to eat and drink

- Change in amount or character of manure or urine

- Refusal to stand/walk

- Refusal to bear weight on a leg

- Puncture wounds

- Wounds with skin edges gaped open

- Difficulty breathing or swallowing

- Heavy bleeding

- Unexplained bleeding from any body orifice

- Depression in a mare several hours after breeding or foaling

Information for the Veterinarian

Should your horse be ill or injured, have answers to the following questions ready when you call the veterinarian:

1. How long has the horse been in this condition?

2. What are the horse's vital signs?
    — pulse, respiration, gum color, temperature.

3. Is the horse eating feed and drinking water?

4. Is the horse urinating and passing manure? Have there been any changes in the manure?

5. Have there been any major changes in the horse's environment, work load or feed in the last 24 to 48 hours (i.e., long trailer ride, just dewormed, new load of hay)?

6. Is the horse bleeding?

7. Has the horse received any treatment so far? If yes, what and how has he responded?

8. Age of the horse.

9. Has the horse been on any medications lately? Is the horse on any medication now?

10. Is the horse exhibiting any unusual behavior (i.e., lying down, attempting to roll, unwilling to put weight on one foot, depressed, etc.)?

First-aid supplies

First-aid supplies to have on hand:

- Peroxide

- Iodine-based surgical soap

- Iodine/Betadine/Povidone solution

- Alcohol

- Large, non-adherent Telfa wound dressings (the larger the better, you can always cut to size)

- 2 rolls of soft, contour-conforming wound dressing – i.e., Webril

- Clean roll cotton and/or quilted stall wraps (keep sealed in a bag)

- Self-adherent elastic leg wrap – i.e., Vetrap

- Extra lead rope (never leaves this spot!)

- Blankets or coolers

- Thermometer

- Wire cutters and sharp knife

- Belt or other suitable tourniquet material

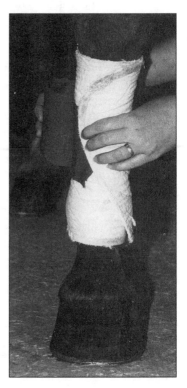

Speak with your veterinarian about the following:

- Antibiotic eye ointment

- Injectable penicillin with supply of needles and syringes or antibiotic in paste form

- Phenylbutazone paste

- Injectable flunixin meglumine in case of colic

Contacts

Amino-Fac
Uckele Animal Health Corp.
800-248-0330
517-486-4341
www.uckele.com

Antioxidant Concentrate
Vita-Key
800-539-8482
940-627-3100
www.vita-key.com

Calf Manna
Manna Pro Corp.
800-821-5984
913-621-2355
www.mannapro.com

CocoSoya
Uckele Animal Health Corp.
800-248-0330
517-486-4341
www.uckele.com

Cough Free
Sure Nutrition
800-789-0146
215-364-4070
www.sure-nutrition.com

Custom Support Foam
3M Animal Care Products
800-848-0829
651-733-8477

Ester C
Select The Best
800-648-0950
775-246-3022
www.selectthebest.com

Mountain Meadow Blend
Montana Pride's
800-531-9682
406-683-6821
www.mtpride.com

Opt-E-Horse
Weaver Leather
800-932-8371
330-674-7548
www.weaverleather.com

Pure C
Vita-Flex Nutrition, Inc.
800-848-2359
802-244-7474
www.vita-flex.com

Ration Plus
Ration Plus for Horses
800-728-4667
804-438-5590
www.rationplus.com

Re-sorb
Pfizer Animal Health
800-733-5500
519-640-6007
www.pfizer.com

Respun Paste and CocoSoya
Uckele Animal Health Corp.
800-248-0330
517-486-4341
www.uckele.com

Wind Aid
Hawthorne Products
800-548-5658
765-768-6585
www.hawthorne-products.com

Index

For information regarding *John Lyons' Perfect Horse*,
the monthly magazine, see our web site www.perfecthorse.com
or call the publisher, Belvoir Publications, Inc. at 800-424-7887.

PHOTO CREDITS: DONNA DIXON-WOODALL, CHARLES HILTON, ISABEL KUREK,
SUE STUSKA, MARK WALPIN, MAUREEN GALLATIN
BOOK DESIGN AND LAYOUT: SUSAN R. TOMKIN